DRUNK LOVE

A Marriage the Under Influence

A MEMOIR BY
**MELISSA
STOELTJE**

This book is a memoir and thus a work of memory. Specific conversations and other details have been recalled or reimagined to the best of my ability; any mistakes or mis-rememberings are solely mine. Names and identifying characteristics of certain individuals have been changed to protect their privacy and preserve their anonymity.

DRUNK LOVE
A Marriage Under the Influence

MELISSA
FLETCHER
STOELTJE

Published by:
Library Tales Publishing
www.LibraryTalesPublishing.com
www.Facebook.com/LibraryTalesPublishing

For general information on our other products and services, please contact our Customer Care Department at 1-800-754-5016, or fax 917-463-0892. For technical support, please visit www.Library-TalesPublishing.com

Library Tales Publishing also publishes its books in a variety of electronic formats. Every content that appears in print is available in electronic books.

ISBN-13:
979-8-89441-015-9

Prologue

The shade lifts from my eyes the moment our car turns onto West Summit Avenue. What had been utter blankness suddenly transformed into a dim gray soup of our neighbors' houses flowing past my window. Newly roused, I try to speak. The trouble is, my tongue won't work. The half-dozen cocktails I've downed over the course of the evening still have a wrestler's grip on my brain's verbal center. My words come out in one long, ridiculous schmear.

My husband, my steadfast drinking buddy, a gentle bear of a man who loves me more than anyone, has finally reached his breaking point.

"Shut up," Mark mutters. "Just shut the fuck up."

The night began with drinks at a dimly lit bar a few blocks away from the Majestic Theater, where we had tickets to see *Jersey Boys*. Mark and I each downed a jumbo martini. He wanted to order a second, but I said no because we were meeting friends for dinner before the show, and I needed to stay on the right side of the slur zone. The last time Mary saw me, I was very drunk. My plan for the evening was to prove to her that I'm not a hopeless lush. To prove it to myself, too.

This goal—to get drunk but not too drunk—has become an increasingly tricky *pas de deux* over the past five years, a development that has stumped both Mark and me. For most of my thirty-plus-year drinking career, I managed my buzz effortlessly, a feat finessed with nary a thought. Nowadays, I'm prone to overshooting the mark, even on nights when my secret vow is to stay within the bounds of respectable inebriation.

Mark and I walk several blocks to the restaurant, where the streets of downtown San Antonio are crowded with curio shops and Hawaiian-shirted tourists. When we get there, Mary and her twenty-something son have already been seated, along with another couple we've never met. We order dinner, and the waiter asks me more than once if I want a wine refill. After three (or four), I lose count.

From there, the night becomes a series of bright camera flashes in a sea of darkness. On the walk to the theater, I'm ticked off because the husband of the couple asked if I was retired, perhaps due to my newly undyed silver hair.

"What the fuck!" I exclaim to Mary's son as we enter the theater. "I mean, look at me!" I gesture to my body. At fifty-two, I'm trim, with a spunky pixie haircut and wire-frame glasses.

"You look good," he says casually, before hurrying to catch up with his mother.

"You're being too loud," Mark whispers in my ear.

Before the lights go down, at my insistence, Mark eases a plastic flute of champagne into my hand. This is when the tape player in my head stops recording. There's a brief flash: I'm waiting in line for the restroom. Mark asks if I want something else to drink.

White wine and a glass of water. Again, darkness. Then, a flash of light at the end of the show: a standing ovation. I hear Mark mutter his standard sarcastic refrain, taken from a *Seinfeld* episode.

"So, we're doing *this* now," he sighs, lifting his big, hulking frame and reluctantly clapping. All the show's singing, dancing, and dialogue—my brain laid down not a whit of it.

This loss of time at the theater represents my first true blackout. Oh, I'd had a few brownouts before: dinner party chatter gone missing, fugitive chunks of movies I'd seen but couldn't recall, but these lapses were easy to explain away. I was just tired—simple as that. A real blackout served as my Maginot Line, the true indicator that my drinking was out of control and that I needed to stop.

At least that's what I told myself.

When we get home from the theater, I lurch into the house, strip off my clothes, and pee. I have the presence of mind to swallow two Advil, as well as the new antidepressant I'm taking for my chronic insomnia, a medication that will figure a month or so down the road in my last few furious dance steps with denial. Mark climbs into bed and turns away from me. Even his back looks angry. Before I slide into sleep, I hear him murmur, "We're going to have to do something about this."

It turns out my husband's plan to "do something" about my drinking wasn't just another of his idle threats, full of sound and fury but fleeting as a summer thunderstorm. What happened the next day would turn my life upside down, a life that, by this point, was a study in paradox and functional duplicity. To the outside world, I'm a successful journalist, a wonderful wife, and a doting mother to an only child. By all public metrics, I'm a loving sister, caring daughter, and law-abiding citizen. But inside our home, my disease is deepening, boiling into a fermenting rot, splashing misery on the two people I love the most: my husband and son.

There are doubtless many women like me—women who drown their tensions, strains, and insecurities every night with goblets of wine (these memes didn't come out of nowhere), then drag their tired bodies and minds to work each day, keeping up appearances and responsibilities. We may not rack up the classic markers of problem drinking—lost jobs, DUIs, titanic blackouts, morning jitters, jail stints—but we're suffering all the same.

And we cause suffering, too. For women like me, the collateral damage of our addiction is the spouses and children we claim to adore—often the only people who see our disease. We are so good at keeping it hidden.

We get away with it because we can.

Fifteen years later, that's only part of the story I'm telling.

In my case, the "getting away with it" ended abruptly the day after my drunken night at the Majestic. Mark made a decision that triggered a true turning point—not just in my drinking career, but in my marriage. You know the old adage, "be careful what you wish for; you just might get it"? Mark wanted a sober wife, and he would get one. What we didn't know was that my putting down the wine glass would unleash a myriad of pathologies that had long bubbled just beneath the surface of our relationship. Sick dynamics that the booze served to tamp down.

There's a reason why most marriages wherein the alcoholic gets sober end up in divorce anyway.

That's another part of the story I'm telling. It's a long, winding journey that can be summed up in a few simple words: Alcohol brought us together. Would my sobriety tear us apart?

But in the decades before I met my husband (and favorite drinking buddy), there were signs—red flares shot into a darkening sky—that suggested drinking might not be a great fit for me. Subtle and sly at first, they became increasingly obvious as the years wore on.

By the end, it was clear that I was a woman in trouble. And my marriage hung in the balance.

PART ONE

WHAT WE WERE LIKE THEN

Chapter One

It's Christmas—or maybe Thanksgiving. Our house is full of relatives—except for my father, who left some years earlier when I was just six. An artist with movie-star looks and a violent temper, he never liked it when my mother's family came around. My memories of him are dim, blurry recollections of Sunday morning trips to the ice house to buy candy, staged to sabotage my mother's plans for church. One memory is crystal clear: the morning my father punched my mother in the face at the breakfast table. She fell to the floor, weeping and clutching her cheek, as my older sister and I cried into our Cocoa Puffs. When my father was in a full rage, my mother would take us into the bathroom, lock the door, and put us in the tub with her while he pounded on the door and screamed obscenities. I don't recall these episodes, but my older sister does. I wouldn't see my father again until my twenties, when the blank space he left behind would be filled with something temporary and unsavory. Even when Jack did live with us, he wasn't around much, spending most of his time at his studio or a bar called the Ebb Tide down the street, where he nurtured his nascent alcoholism, the warped genes he passed down to me, his middle daughter.

Father gone, we still live in the home my parents built, a Frank Lloyd Wright-style house full of modular 60s furniture and paintings on every wall. Two large A-frame windows flank the living room. Birds sometimes fly into them, and my sisters and I find their stiff bodies lying in the grass next to the house.

Like my siblings, I have a bowl haircut that my mother cuts in her bathroom, holding the comb in her teeth as she carefully clips straight-across bangs. We can't afford a real hairdresser on the meager pay she earns as a freelance fashion artist. (Jack pays child support, but only the minimum; he told the judge he needed most of his money for art supplies.) She works late into the night, hunched over an easel in her bedroom, where she coaxes ladies in fancy hats and sleek shoes onto onion skin paper with slim paintbrushes and India ink.

Today, the house is full of smells like cinnamon and onion, and the windows steam up from pie baking. My mother's cheeks are flushed with color. "Who wants a sip of wine?"

How old am I? Eight? Nine? I know I'm young—these little sips are a family tradition. I step forward, open my mouth like a baby bird. The wine is cloyingly sweet and syrupy. It's full and round in my mouth. It burns a little going down but leaves a lovely fruit-tinged coating in my throat. The sip slides to my stomach, where it nestles, curled and warm.

This, I think, *is something special.*

My mother, a former model with a long, elegant neck and dark hair twisted into a chignon, is a true social drinker, indulging in the occasional highball. By the time I'm ten, she works as the advertising manager at Dillard's, a job with long, hard hours and seemingly never enough pay. She comes home at night exhausted and on edge, snapping if one of us accidentally overturns a glass of iced tea at dinner. However, she rarely drinks during the week.

My mother keeps her home bar well-stocked. The bottles reside in a cabinet near our kitchen, a small battalion of shapes and colors: brown bourbon, crystal-clear Smirnoff, emerald green crème de menthe, and the luscious jewel tones of sherries and cordials. I can't remember how old I am when she starts letting me mix her weekend whiskey sours. The process holds a stately grandeur: a squat cocktail glass filled with ice, a measure of Jim Beam poured in the elegant silver jigger then splashed over the ice, the sharp medicinal scent wafting upwards into my nose. A quick shake of the mixer, a good stir, and then the finishing touch: two bright red maraschino cherries.

I'm in my early teens when my mother invites me to join her at cocktail hour. I always add a touch more bourbon to my glass than to hers. Sitting next to her in our living room recliners, sipping and watching the evening news, I feel the tight coils within me gradually loosening. The jittery molecules that are constantly zinging and zipping around my body settle down. I feel a delicious ache in my hip bones and think: *This. This is how I'm supposed to feel.*

My first real drunken episode happens on a cold winter night at a friend's house two blocks over from mine. Her parents are out of town, though I keep this fact from my mother. "I'll pick you up at ten," she says. She doesn't want me walking home in the dark. My mother is a worrier. I am still in middle school.

The party is happening in a converted backyard garage, and everyone is there: my friend, her older brothers, and a clutch of neighborhood kids. There's a pool table, blacklight posters on the wall, a waterbed, and Led Zeppelin blaring on the stereo. Cigarette smoke clouds the darkened room.

"You want a beer?" one of the brothers asks. He's tall and rangy, acne pockmarks studding his face.

"Yes, please."

He swings open the door of a dented refrigerator, and in the flash of light, I see a case or two, something cheap, like Schlitz. I pop open the top, and the fizzy *swish!* sounds like emancipation. The first beer goes down cold and bubbly. Within moments, my personality transforms. I stop caring what the other kids think of me. Soon, I'm the big shot, cracking jokes with the older kids, playing pool, missing every shot and not giving a damn. Someone turns the stereo louder. The music thrums in my head, pounds in my chest:

Want a whole-lotta-love. Want-a-whole-lotta-love. Want-a-whole-lotta-love.

The night grows fuzzy. I'm not feeling so good. My friend leads me, stumbling, into her bedroom in the main house. She helps me up the ladder to the top bunk. I sprawl on my back and shut my eyes, the world doing its famous drunken spinning. The heater must be cranked on full blast. Waves of warm air blanket me as I fade in and out of consciousness, my wet shirt sticking to my back when I turn over. Then someone is jostling my shoulder. "Your mother is out front." I walk unsteadily to her car, praying I don't reek of beer. The cold air hits me like a tonic.

"I don't feel so good," I say, sliding in.

My mother puts her hand on my forehead.

"You feel pretty hot," she says. "Let's get you home."

In the bathroom, I peel off my damp shirt and barely make it to the toilet before the retching starts. The beer is far less tasty coming up than it was going down, and it fills the bowl with a sour, amber foam flecked with that night's dinner.

"You must have a virus," my mother says from the other side of the door.

She and I have a fractious relationship. Of her three daughters, I resemble her detested ex-husband the most, from my brown eyes to the shape of my nose. It sometimes feels like everything I do irritates her—like I'm a nuisance, my very existence a bother. She may be more powerful than me, still willing to use her brown belt on my bare ass at times, but I'm devious, always finding ways to subvert her authority with passive aggression.

Make no mistake: deep down, I know my mother loves me and would take a bullet for me. She can be loving and fun, laughing on the couch as my sisters and I dance crazily around the living room to a wild xylophone album. Life would be so much easier if people were either all good or all bad.

Tonight, my mom's nurturing side comes out, the one that never fails to emerge when any of us are sick. She's being the warm washcloth mom, the chicken soup mom tonight. A sense of guilt intensifies my nausea. I curl above the porcelain bowl, coughing up mouthfuls of brackish foam, and make a vow: I will never drink too much again.

Let's call this red flare number one.

Chapter Two

That vow is one I would break multiple times in high school—but with less vomiting.

Not long after the garage party, I meet Vanessa, the girl who would become my best friend in middle school, and together we embark on grand adventures in illicit substances. A transplant from Alaska, she's a pretty brunette who quickly becomes the most popular girl in school. Why she picked me, a virtual nobody, to become her partner in crime is a mystery. I make her laugh, I guess, and Vanessa loves to laugh. It's a tumbling, bubbling sound that becomes like a drug to me. A fellow product of a broken home, she's riddled with insecurities despite an outward display of bravado and flirting, and she's always on the hunt for ways to change how she feels. In this, we were a perfect match.

As eighth graders, we start with pot and, of course, alcohol: Boone's Farm apple wine or whatever else we can pilfer from her mother's refrigerator or mine. Occasionally, we get the older guys Vanessa knows to buy alcohol for us. By high school, we've graduated to mescaline and LSD, which is fun until it's not; a few bad trips pour gasoline on the panic attacks I began having freshman year. They start with my becoming hyper-aware of my breathing. Within seconds, I can't breathe normally: a vise grips my chest, my hands grow slippery, my heart thuds against my ribs. The attacks happen most often in class, where I'm trapped, a wild animal caught in a cage. The most frightening part of these episodes is that I don't know when they'll strike. Soon, the mere thought of one is enough to set the whole nightmare into motion.

I don't tell anyone about what's happening. Obviously, I am going mad. But to the outside world, to my high school comrades, I look just fine. I'm bone-skinny, with scrawny arms and legs, the thinness of which I accentuate by pegging my bell-bottom blue jeans extra tight around the thighs. All the girls do it. Our jeans have one-inch zippers and ride low on our hips. In accordance with the current style, my brown hair is long, straight, and parted in the middle. I have braces and high cheekbones. As is the trend, I eschew makeup and bra-wearing—a holdover from the sixties. In my case, it doesn't matter much, as I'm humiliatingly flat. I wear flowery Mexican peasant shirts. I look like a flower child—or maybe a Manson girl.

Early in high school, I find my tribe: all the other misbegotten youth from broken homes or dysfunctional homes or perhaps just unfortunate gene pools. We're troubled water seeking its own level. We hang out together before school, smoking cigarettes and joints at a nearby convenience store, where I flirt with boys who will wind up in jail or an early grave or God knows where. By sophomore year, some of us walk to a wooded area not far from school, where we tie off each other's arms and inject crystal meth. I only do it a half-dozen times—and I only let Vanessa shoot me up. The speed zooms up your spine like hot wax and cracks open your brain—an explosion of ecstatic bumblebees that vibrate in your body and mind for hours. Believe it or not, it feels *good*.

Throughout my undistinguished high school career, I had various school suspensions for skipping out and assorted juvenile delinquent malfeasance. I break curfew constantly, run away to Port Aransas for spring break, and otherwise bedevil my increasingly furious mother. She blames most of it on Vanessa. She hates Vanessa, believing she's a bad influence. She's right; I would follow Vanessa into any dark corner she chose.

But by senior year, my best friend is gone, ejected from MacArthur High and sent to an alternative school. I've hardly acquitted myself as a student, but have amassed enough credits to enroll in a vocational program, leaving campus at noon to work in the men's underwear department at Sears.

Day after day, I stand under ghastly fluorescent lights, folding and refolding undershirts, ringing up fuzzy old grandmothers who buy crew socks for their grandsons, willing the hours to pass. The roasting popcorn kernels from the nearby snack kiosk impart a perpetual movie-lobby smell. I feel like I'm constantly coated in fake butter. Some days, when my boss orders me to redo the boxer end cap, I picture myself taking a handgun and blowing my brain to bits.

But everything changes once I meet Antonio. Tall and skinny, he works in men's suits across the aisle. A year older than me, he has slithery hips and black kinky hair. Picture a Hispanic Lionel Richie.

Antonio likes to dance disco, so we dress up in polyester outfits and hit various dance floors around town, shimmying to Donna Summer and KC and the Sunshine Band. Antonio also likes to drink sugary Seagram's and 7-Up, but since he's a good Catholic boy, we don't do drugs.

We have sex frequently on the red fake-leather back seat of my '66 Mercury Comet or against the side of his house, where he still lives with his parents, after I drop him off following a night of dancing.

I lost my virginity early in high school, to an older guy I met through Vanessa. It took repeated painful attempts on his part before my body finally unclenched and let him in. (I'll later learn that there's a term for this: vaginismus, a condition that can indicate prior sexual trauma). After a night of copious tequila intake, we finally completed the act. Mysteriously, I didn't bleed.

Antonio and I get drunk, but it's all at acceptable levels of late seventies disco-era drunk. I don't do anything stupid—that is, until the last night we're together.

I'm due to leave for college. Even with my middling grades, I managed to get into a mediocre public university up the road in San Marcos, somehow placing out of freshman English with my ACT scores (*What?*). On our last date in San Antonio—we pledge to stay together despite the distance, but won't—Antonio and I get wasted on Seagram's. With the pristine logic of the inebriated, I decide to sneak him into my bedroom after a late night at the disco. We disrobe and start having sex on the carpeted floor between the two twin beds. Suddenly, a sliver of hallway light shines through the crack under the door. I push him off me. "Quick, get under the bed!" A second or so later, my mother turns on the bedroom light. "Hey," I slur, pulling my dress in front of myself. "What's going on?" she asks, her face clouded with sleep. "Nothing," I say. She peers deeper into the room, and there, sticking out from under the bed, are Antonio's oversized brown feet.

"What are you *doing*?" my mother whispers furiously. "Get him *out* of here!" She scuttles back to bed.

To my amazement, there are no recriminations the next day, no consequences. By then, my mother had been married to her second husband, a research scientist with a binge-drinking problem, for about a year. I try to give my stepfather a wide berth, especially when he's had a few drinks and his eyes take on a creepy, glassy look. Perhaps my mother didn't want to rile him up with news of my transgression. He and I already weren't on the best of terms. He couldn't wait for me to get out of the house.

I look in the mirror that morning, hungover, with black streaks of mascara under my eyes. *What was I thinking, bringing a guy into my childhood bedroom?* For a moment,

I know the truth: I hadn't been thinking at all. The whiskey had been in full control of my prefrontal cortex. For a few seconds, I'm awash in self-loathing. *How different, really, was I from my stepfather? A man who said and did things while drunk that made me afraid of him, that repulsed me?*

I push the thought away and start packing for college.

Red flare number two.

Chapter Three

Southwest Texas State University is a college on a hill, known for its hard-partying students and the San Marcos River, a spring-fed, pristine waterway that dissects the quaint town. The first thing I notice is the plethora of beautiful blonde sorority girls, who strut around campus as if they own the place—which I'm pretty sure they do. Next to them, I'm a homely brown raisin.

I need to earn my own spending money in college, so I take a job as a cocktail waitress at The Restless Wind, a dive bar within walking distance from my dormitory. The atmosphere is dark and dank, permeated by the smell of stale beer and cigarettes, with pool tables in the back and country music playing on the jukebox. Each evening, the bar fills up with regulars, mostly townsfolk who bear the hard-edged look of years of heavy drinking. The preferred drink is Johnny Walker Black with a splash. While everyone is polite enough to me, it's often in a distracted manner—I'm simply the delivery system. Weekends tend to get rowdy; occasional fights break out, and couples sometimes retreat to the bathroom for intimacy. However, any hurt feelings seem to dissipate quickly—by Monday, everyone is back in good spirits, drinking, smoking, joking, and slapping each other on the back. I begin to realize, somewhat hazily, that many of my customers are alcoholics. I reassure myself: as much as I enjoy drinking, I'm determined never to end up like them. *No way.*

My roommate is a sweet girl named Mandy from the Rio Grande Valley—a corn-fed, angelic girl with a halo of curly hair and aviator glasses. She's a virgin in every sense of the word. She's never even tried a cigarette, let alone gotten drunk. Early in the semester, I convince her to take a walk on the wild side. The drinking age is still eighteen. We buy a bottle of bourbon, a six-pack of Coca-Cola, and a pack of Marlboro Lights. We wedge a towel under the dorm door. I mix our drinks and then sit back to enjoy the show.

"Man, this is making me dizzy," Mandy says after a few sips.

"Just give it a chance," I nudge. She coughs from the cigarette and decides it's better if she doesn't inhale (I think, *where's Vanessa when I need her?*). We get pretty toasted that night, but Mandy decides she doesn't like the way it makes her feel in class the next day (*What a wuss!*). We bring the bottle out a few more times on weekend nights, and then it's gone, and we don't buy another. Mandy's mother sends her packages filled with homemade cookies and brownies, and I often sneak some for myself, gobbling them down in secret in the bathroom. Before I know it, I've packed on thirty pounds.

I started binge eating with a girlfriend my senior year of high school, the two of us stuffing ourselves with candy and junk food after school. I continued the habit on my own, consuming anything high-calorie in our kitchen pantry (which would prompt from my mother, "What happened to all the cookies?"). Some days I'd eat until I was sick. Other days, I'd subsist on apples and diet soda, going to bed with excruciating headaches, wondering if Aspirin had any calories. Unlike my friend and many other girls in the eating disorder sorority, I could never force myself to barf. Early in my first year of college, my bingeing worsens. Soon, I can't even look in my dorm room mirror, appalled by my bloated, chipmunk face, engulfed in self-hatred.

The lead-up to my sophomore year starts out a little more hopefully. I'd lost some weight over the summer. A friend from high school calls, asking if I want to room with her for the upcoming year in San Marcos. Madeline has the perfect body—big boobs, tiny waist—and thick, tawny hair. She's a bit on the prim side, a little prissy, but she's nice, and we'd partied together in high school. My mother has already told me I'm on my own from here on out, both for tuition payments and living costs. Since I have no other housing options, I agree to room with Madeline.

We put off finding a place until summer is almost over. The only rentable space we can find is a dilapidated trailer near the back of a third-rate mobile home park on the outskirts of town. It becomes clear early on that I'm going to be living solo: Madeline spends most of her time at her boyfriend's house. The trailer is in such bad shape that it had been slated to become a laundromat, until we signed the lease. The linoleum is peeling from the floor, the appliances are battered and ancient, and the lock on the hallway door that opens to the outside is broken. Every night, I jam a chair under the handle to dissuade intruders.

I get a waitressing job at a natural foods restaurant that's walking distance from the trailer park. That's where I meet Joey. He's a cook there and also a fellow college student. He's wiry and short and impish, a ponytailed leprechaun. Like Antonio, Joey likes to party (you could say I have a type). He also has a line on Quaaludes, those mega-downers popular in the seventies that turn you into a human Gumby. One night, after quaffing beer from the restaurant's kegs and downing Quaaludes, Joey lets me drive his yellow Camaro. I end up driving it into a ditch, and we have to call a wrecker. Joey is so downed-out that he doesn't even get mad at me.

It's understood that he and I are just having fun. At least, that's the impression I get. We're wastoids together. Fuck buddies. One night, we're drinking in the trailer, a night that sets off another red flag. I don't recall if we've taken Quaaludes, but given what happens, I sort of hope it wasn't just alcohol clouding my judgment.

Joey and I sit on the ratty living room sofa, drinking beer. It's around midnight, and we're both sloshed. Unexpectedly, my roommate Madeline walks through the door. Joey has mentioned that he finds her hot. She and her boyfriend have had a fight, so she wants to sleep in her own bed instead of staying at his place. She pops open a beer and sits at the kitchen dinette across from us. Then Joey brings up the idea of us having a three-way.

"Are you crazy?" she asks incredulously, looking at Joey, then giving me a hard stare.

Oh, he's serious alright.

"I've always been attracted to you."

I want to please Joey so he won't leave me. At least that's what I tell myself.

"Yeah, come on, let's do it!" I say. "What are you afraid of? Come on, come on, come on!"

Madeline gets up, stalks to her bedroom, and slams the door. The lock makes an audible click. Joey and I eventually pass out in my closet-sized bedroom. In the morning, we don't talk about what had transpired the night before. After he leaves, I find a note on the kitchen dinette from my roommate, informing me her boyfriend wants to meet outside his afternoon class.

Later that day, I trudge to the appointed classroom and peek inside. Dread percolates in my viscera. I can barely believe how I acted the night before. *That wasn't me!* The boyfriend spots me, gets up from his desk and rolls toward the hallway, nothing but rich, frat-boy confidence. He's a golden-haired trust-fund baby with a sports car who favors starched Polo shirts. He and Madeline are forever fighting over his alleged infidelities. When he gets to me, he stands very close, peering down, his aquiline nostrils flaring.

"What you did last night was wrong," he says, a proclamation from Mount Olympus.

"I know," I say. "I'm sorry; I was really drunk." Students from the class are filtering out from the classroom, looking at us.

"That's no excuse," he says. "If it happens again, you're out of the trailer."

"It won't. I promise."

That night, I take a scalding hot shower, but it doesn't wash off the residue of shame. Along with the growing sense that perhaps I can't trust myself when I drink. It takes me three beers to drown out the feeling.

I don't see much of Madeline the rest of the semester. By the year's end, she's transferred to UT Austin. Not long after the threesome incident, Joey and I break up. Not that we were ever much of a couple to begin with. A few other drunken one-night stands follow, but they amount to nothing but morning-after remorse.

At the restaurant, I'm surrounded by food. Sometimes I stand in the walk-in cooler and finger the remnants of a diner's uneaten crab casserole, cramming it into my mouth with an urgency I don't even understand. My double chins have returned, and my pants don't fit. One night, as I'm rounding a corner in the kitchen, my hip hits a tray of silverware, and the contents clatter to the floor. One of the line cooks yells, "*Moooooo!*" All the other cooks burst out laughing.

I smile and laugh along, dying inside.

*　　　*　　　*

At Burgundy Woods, a discotheque in San Antonio where I'll take on my summer waitressing job before my junior year of college, hardly anybody has a sense of shame about anything. Cocaine and crystal meth have everyone running ten feet ahead of their own consciences, with no time to look back. Closing time is when the fun really begins: more lines of meth and then shots of peppermint schnapps lined up on the bar, the staff downing them in unison. The party continues at someone's apartment, drinking and drinking until the sky outside turns dishwater gray. Then everyone climbs into their cars for the perilous journey home, sometimes stopping at Jim's Coffee Shop for a drunken breakfast of eggs and hash browns, our shimmering disco clothes clashing with the sober attire of early-morning workers. Daytime is for sleeping it off. Night comes, and the cycle begins again.

With all the drugs, I'm skinny again. My hip bones jut out from my frame. Burgundy Woods is where I meet Jake, the control freak who will become my first real boyfriend. I don't know about his controlling tendencies yet. He's just the handsome bouncer whose green eyes lock onto mine when I tromp through the disco door in my stilettos, hot pants, and halter top.

Jake likes to smoke pot. He's a former debate champ at the high school we both attended, a year ahead of me. A tall redhead who tends to over-enunciate his words, it's established early on that he is scary smart and the more intelligent one of our duo.

Drunk and vibrating with coke, we hook up one night on a couch on the disco's upper floor, the tawdry start of our years-long relationship.

Jake is an expert water skier. We drive to Lake McQueeney with his high school buddy who owns a boat. When Jake stands up on his skis out of the water, biceps bulging and the sun glancing off his mane of copper hair, he looks like King Neptune rising out of the sea. At summer's end, he promises to visit me at UT Austin, where I have also transferred.

And Jake fulfills his promise. But it turns out he doesn't really like to drink all that much—the summer was false advertising. When he visits, he smokes pot constantly, and we argue and have sex. Occasionally, he'll buy a bottle of gin and we'll have gin-and-tonics. But it's not enough.

I live in a three-bedroom rental in a leafy part of Austin with two guys I vaguely knew from high school. They're more friends of Jake's than mine; it's how I found a place to live. Both are UT students; one is also a part-time drug dealer. From time to time, the house fills with the stink of feces from a broken sewage line. We also have a bad roach infestation; turn the kitchen light on at night and it's like the whole room moves.

There's a convenience store across the street, which is indeed convenient, because by now I've gotten in the habit of buying a tallboy beer or two every night. It's all I can afford on my work-study and waitressing jobs. I count out my change on the store counter, the cashier watching me impatiently. At this point, if I don't have at least some alcohol every night, all's not right with the world. I don't question this growing need of mine: *Don't all college students drink?*

It's in this rental home that a cardinal event occurs, one almost every alcoholic will recognize: the first time someone comments on their drinking.

It's a weeknight. I sit in the den on the scratchy, half-circle couch, my feet propped up on the coffee table, watching *Full House*, an ignored psychology textbook open on my lap. Tonight, the house is only at mid-stink level. I've eaten my poor college student's meal of fake-orange macaroni and cheese. I'm draining the final suds of my tallboy beer. One of my roommates, the drug dealer, walks into the room. He's a big, former football player who snorts cocaine on most weekends, occasionally sharing some with me.

"There you go," he says, mimicking the way I hold the can aloft.

I pause mid-swallow and bring the can down to my lap.

"That's right," I say, wearily.

"I notice you drink every night, huh?" He's got a sly smile on his face.

"Yeah, I guess." I stare back at him, feeling the need to explain myself but also knowing it will only make me appear more culpable. "Not always."

"OK. Interesting."

He retreats into the kitchen to make a sandwich. A tiny caution flag unfurls in my head: *Why did he feel the need to comment on my drinking? And why does it make me uneasy?*

Years later, it will make for a good anecdote in 12-Step meetings: When a drug dealer comments on your drinking, you may have a problem.

Chapter Four

I decide that I can't live without Jake, even with all the fighting in our relationship and his abstemiousness around alcohol. So, I transfer to UT San Antonio for my senior year and move into his efficiency apartment, even though he never formally asked me to. The complex is an aging, squat beige box plopped along a busy boulevard on a shabby, rundown side of town. The apartment is drab and utilitarian, except for the row of empty Riesling wine bottles that line the headboard of Jake's bed (more false advertising). The people who live in the complex are mostly poor. A man with schizophrenia who rents the corner apartment on the third floor sometimes hangs out on the landing, naked, gesticulating, and yelling strange things until the police, who are eventually called, arrive.

I get a job waitressing at an Indian restaurant at a strip center across the street that is a combination Italian delicatessen. When I breeze in through the glass front door for my shift, the air is redolent with peppers and salami and basmati rice. I wear the same long, flowery dress every night; whenever I iron it, the lingering scent of curry wafts up into my nose. It's kind of a partying place. The cooks, the owners—we all drink. As closing time nears, we fill red plastic tea glasses with the cheap wine the restaurant sells. Jake is usually asleep when I get home, so he doesn't smell it on my breath. He doesn't really approve of my drinking. He's incredibly cheap, and alcohol costs money. Except for what I drink at work, and what I'm "allowed" to drink with Jake on the weekends, when he parties with his buddies, my habit essentially goes underground for a year or so. Here's the strange thing about alcoholism, at least for me: it can do weird things like that. It can morph and subside and reemerge, keeping you guessing as to whether you actually have a problem.

The Big Book of the 12-Step fellowship for problem drinkers describes alcohol as "cunning, baffling, and powerful."

About two years in, I get fed up with our constricted lifestyle. A good time for Jake means sitting on the bed in his apartment, smoking pot and watching shows on his small black-and-white portable TV, after a meal of chipped beef on toast or fake crab cakes and instant mashed potatoes. Jake's mother buys groceries for him on the cheap at the military commissary. He is such a tightwad that, on the rare occasions when we do go out to eat (with a coupon, of course), he makes me smuggle a carton of sour cream in my purse instead of splurging on buying a side of it to dump on my enchiladas.

It says a lot about my own self-regard at the time that I went along with all this abnegation willingly. More troublesome: our bickering was beginning to take on physical tones. I slapped him once during a fight, and he slapped me back, hard. He almost made me get out of his vintage green Mustang on a bad side of town until I apologized for some transgression.

Things are about to change. By happenstance, I sign up for an assertiveness seminar at one of my mother's women empowerment workshops. She'd discovered feminism at mid-life. By now, she's in full-blown activist mode, having been able to quit her wretched advertising job and pursue women's liberation work, funded by my stepfather's paycheck. Buoyed by the workshop's insights, I finally find my courage and break up with Jake.

But not before I get a brief window of insight, once again, into the places drinking can take me.

When our relationship is on its last legs, my thirst reemerges in a big way, energized by its period of hibernation, leading to a second cardinal event in my addiction journey: my first 12-Step meeting.

Jake has an out-of-town assignment. He's started a new job and must attend a weekend training program. When he kisses me goodbye and heads down the stairs, I'm liberated. *Free at last!* The first thing I do is call Vanessa.

"He's gone. Let's party."

We go to a strip mall bar. There are four of us, clustered around a table on the rim of the dance floor. Tequila shots commence. I can't get the alcohol down fast enough. I notice an attractive guy behind the bar and recognize that he's someone I went to high school with. As he walks by our table, I grab his hand. It turns out he's the assistant manager. He remembers me and smiles.

"Dance with me," I say.

We slow dance. He smells good, like pine-scented wood chips.

We're about to kiss when I let it slip that I live with Jake, my boyfriend.

"Wait, what?" He stops dancing and pushes me to arm's length. It appears they were high school friends, too.

"But he's out of town," I say, slurring a bit.

"No way. Won't do it to a friend."

"But I hate Jake," I say to his retreating back.

I'm mortified. So, I do more shots. And more shots. The song "Shout!" comes on, and Vanessa pulls me onto the dance floor. When it gets to the part where everyone is supposed to shimmy low to the ground, I do my drunken best, but I fall over. Flat on my ass. I try it a second time and fall again. The other dancers laugh at me.

When my eyes fly open the next morning, shame is already lodged in my chest, squatting like a fat toad. *Oh no! I came on to the assistant manager! What if he tells Jake? Oh my God, I fell down on the dance floor—twice.*

I bolt up from bed, grab the phone book, and flip to the listing for 12-Step meetings in San Antonio. The passing fears I'd entertained since high school were suddenly coalescing into something real. Something urgent. The phone rings in my ear. A woman answers, sounding inappropriately cheery.

"I think I might have a problem," I say.

"Would you like to go to a meeting?"

Do I want to go to a meeting? I don't want to go to a meeting.

"Yes. I think."

"OK sweetie. Just give me your address, and I'll pick you up tonight."

I stand by the dumpster in the apartment parking lot as the sun descends, shooting Dreamsicle-orange rays of light across a pearly sky. A guy pulls into a nearby parking space in his dented hooptie, gets out, and nods at me as he passes by. I nod back. His skin is sallow, dabbed with scab marks, a few teeth missing. Meth?

Little cracks of resistance begin to appear. *Was my behavior really that bad? I'm not the only woman who's tried to step out on her boyfriend. And who hasn't fallen down on the dance floor?* I'm about to hightail it back to the apartment when a battered old Ford pulls up.

"Hey darlin'! Climb on in."

An older woman with silver locks piled in curlicues atop her head smiles at me through the open passenger window. She's frumpy, like somebody's Appalachian grandmother. Baggy floral-print dress, bright orange lipstick. She leans over and pushes the passenger door wide open.

"Come on, sweetie pie. I don't bite."

I slide in next to her, feeling prickles of sweat on the back of my neck. We're headed to a place called Club 12, the de facto headquarters of 12-Step programs in San Antonio. I steal furtive glances at my chauffeur as we speed down the highway. There are rips in the car's upholstery, through which bits of foam are poking out.

"So, tell me about your drinking," she says.

Oh, Jesus. Where do I start?

"Well, I do like to drink. Sometimes a little too much. I think I might be a little bit of an alcoholic."

The woman throws her head back and cackles.

"Oh, darlin'. That's like being a little bit pregnant. You either are or you aren't."

Club 12 turns out to be a normal-looking building that has seen better days. The meeting takes place in a big room, lit up like an airplane hangar and crowded with chairs and people. The air holds the acrid scent of multiple overheated coffee pots. Everyone looks normal, not a skid-row bum in the bunch. For a split second, I'm terrified I will see someone I know. A quick survey of the room reveals no familiar faces. Most attendees are decades older than me.

To start the meeting, everyone intones something called the Serenity Prayer, a chant about accepting things you can't change, blah blah. It all sounds pretty cultish to me. Group chants give me the heebie-jeebies (unless it's at a football game). I try to pay attention, but it all sounds like gobble-dygook: "God" and "powerlessness" and "a desire to stop drinking." I have no desire to stop drinking, really. I just want to never embarrass myself again.

When it's over, everyone stands in a circle to join hands and recite the Lord's Prayer (I'm thinking, *holy shit, this really isn't the place for me, I gave up on religion in high school*). I stand in the corner and wait for Minnie Pearl, who's chatting up friends, to give me a ride home. A young woman, one of the few closer to my age, approaches me. She's toying with a packet of Sweet 'N Low, folding and refolding the tiny pink square. She smiles warmly at me. *What's with these people and all the smiling?*

"I've never seen you here before," she says. "Is this your first meeting?"

"Yeah." I'm not really in the mood for chit-chat. I want to get the hell out of Dodge. But I was raised to be polite, so I beam back at her, pretending to be all interested in being saved.

"When did you stop drinking?"

My smile fades for a microsecond. *Is this some sort of test?*

"Yesterday."

I detect a fleeting look of confusion on the young woman's face. *Is she wondering how I can look this good the day after I stopped drinking? I'm not shaking, I'm not bloated, I'm not disgusting.* Surely that's what she's thinking. *Surely, I don't belong here.*

I'll ride this delusion for years. That's how denial works: a seconds-long look on a stranger's face twisted into proof-positive that a problem doesn't exist. No one ever accuses alcoholics of not being crafty. We will protect and coddle our right to drink to the very gates of Hell.

The next day, Minnie Pearl leaves a voicemail asking if I want to go to another meeting. I don't return her call. She doesn't call again.

But the memory of that first recovery meeting, the *feel* of it, the way the people laughed and seemed so at home in their world, in their own skin, will lodge like a seedling in my brain. There, it will lurk and lay dormant until it's time to germinate and reemerge once again into my life.

Chapter Five

The final fight with Jake is over money. (Surprise!) It's Christmas. I've hardly made any tips in recent weeks at the Indian restaurant. Jake is making decent pay at his government gig. Could he cover my half of the rent this month, so I can buy presents for my family? Sorry, babe. Not gonna do it. I know from my assertiveness class that Jake is *not* on my side. Our last conflagration is one for the ages. I throw my suitcase in the backseat of my rusted-out Cutlass and tear out of the apartment complex parking lot.

I move back in with my mother and stepfather and get a job as a receptionist at a family-owned oil company. But a few weeks in, my living situation blows up. One night, my stepfather comes home from work, roaring drunk and ranting incoherently. It's hard to understand his words—something about how I'm now Jake's common-law wife and should move back in with him. My mother kicks him out—literally kicks him out the front door with her foot. Then she weeps in the front yard, her face in her hands, begging me not to leave as I again throw my suitcase into my rusted-out Cutlass and speed out of the driveway. (My mother and stepfather later reconcile. Somehow this all ends up being my fault. I'm told to apologize to my stepfather. I refuse.)

I move in with my grandmother, a sweet woman whose house had been a refuge for me during childhood. All is peaceful for about a month as I save money to get my own place. I find a one-bedroom apartment on the third floor of one of those interchangeable complexes that hug noisy highways in cities everywhere. I don't have much furniture beyond a bed and a dresser. I put a beanbag chair in one corner and create a bookshelf out of plywood and cinder blocks. My apartment is at the very back of the complex, with a narrow balcony that overlooks the residential neighborhood of modest homes. After work, with a glass of wine, I stand on the balcony and gaze at the tree-dotted backyards and feel irretrievably lonely and strangely homesick. *Will I ever have a home of my own? A sanctuary I won't have to leave? A husband, and maybe children, who love me as I am?* The wine only deepens my self-pity.

I feel the need to drink because I work for a mercurial boss. That's what I tell myself. My supervisor at the oil company is Dan, the head of accounting. After several months, he takes me off the receptionist desk, where the job of answering phones is easy, and makes me his personal assistant. Now, I'm charged with balancing the personal spreadsheets of the young male scions who run the firm, sending checks to the country club for their gin-heavy lunches and other finance-related tasks—or at least, I try to. I'm terrible at my job. I recently graduated from UT San Antonio with an English degree, ready to become the next great American novelist. But the expected fame hasn't materialized—not that I ever sit down and actually *write anything*—so I pass my days typing and punching numbers into a calculator.

When I screw up, which is often, Dan goes into a rage— his pudgy face turning bright red, his thick fish lips huffing and puffing. The young princes who are his bosses routinely underperform as well, but Dan can hardly vent his rage at them, so it trickles down—or rather, spews down—to me. Once, when I'm late coming back from a Friday afternoon wine-heavy lunch with two other secretaries, he pounds the wall with his fist, right in front of me. I spend a lot of my time in a bathroom stall, having panic attacks, which have returned in full force. Over time, I develop a permanent lump in my throat when I swallow. A doctor prescribes me a muscle relaxer, but the pills only serve to turbo-charge my panic attacks. One day, as I'm leaving work, walking down a long hallway of the oil company lobby with the drug in my system, I think I hear someone call my name. I turn and no one is there. Ice water tingles up my spine. The auditory hallucination (if that's what it is) throws me into an out-of-body panic attack that lasts for four days, during which I can barely eat.

I'm falling apart.

Post-Jake, there have been a few suitors. Mostly shrimpy guys who make my thighs look huge in comparison when I sit next to them. On some of these dates, out of nervousness, I drink too much. One date looks at me with blatant disgust when I slur my words toward the end of the night. I never hear from him again.

Being free of Jake's tight rein means I can drink as much as I want. Which, at this point in my twenty-five-year-old life, entails several glasses of wine each night, to unwind from my job, to be able to go to sleep unbothered by the sounds of possible rapists lurking on the stairwell outside my bedroom window. I often drink more on the weekends, and I'm also back to occasional binge eating. My twenties have turned into a debacle, and I wonder: *Is this the tread-mill my life is going to be? Working at a job I hate? Feeling lonely and unloved? Becoming the consummate failure I've always suspected I was?*

Then a miracle happens, although I won't know it's a miracle until much later. I'm about to be given the rest of my life.

But before that, a last word about my panic attacks. Sitting one afternoon in the dentist's office, I read an article about anxiety disorders in *Glamour* magazine. I discover that these attacks don't mean I'm going insane and that they aren't going to kill me. After that, whenever I feel a panic attack coming on, I taunt it. I silently repeat a mantra: *Come on, panic, do your worst. I am not afraid of you. Fuck you.* Somehow, over time, this attitude causes the attacks to shrivel in intensity and finally slink off to the hell from whence they came, never to return.

Now, the miracle. I go to a wedding shower. It's Madeline's, my former roommate in San Marcos. (No, she didn't marry the cheating boyfriend, and yes, she apparently forgave my indiscretion.) Another friend from high school attends. Her face lights up when I tell her I'm still single. Would I like to meet a cute guy who works with her husband at a cable installation company? He's super nice. How about a blind date? Sure, I say. Why not?

Two nights later, I'm standing in the bathroom of my apartment applying smoky eye shadow with one hand while the other holds a flashlight. The power is out, and I'm getting ready for a blind date in near darkness. (If this were a novel, this would be too on-the-nose, but I swear it's true.) I put down the eye shadow and pick up the blush, sweeping color onto my wide cheekbones. Too much color? It's hard to tell in the circle of blue-white light.

I'm a long way from my high school wraith days. I still have shoulder-length brown hair, but now I curl it sometimes. Makeup is obviously back in the picture. Even with the occasional food binges, I'm a respectable size nine. But like many women, I'm insecure about my body. I worry that my stomach pooches out too much. I'm not fond of my breasts, which are no longer flat but still fall far short of spectacular. Basically, I'm passable. Unlike Vanessa, conversations never stop when I enter a room. I've had my share of male attention, sure. But heads don't turn.

I tell myself I don't care if the evening works out. *If this date doesn't take*, I think, *I'm done with men. I'll get a cat.*

I finish with my makeup and feel my way through the dark living room to get my purse, past the ratty Salvation Army couch and the garage sale dinette. I take a deep breath as I lock the door and gaze out from my third-floor landing. It's a crisp January evening, the blue dome of sky shading into azure, the trees bare-limbed in the backyards beyond my apartment. The chill in the air mimics the frisson of anticipation I feel in my stomach. Twenty minutes later, I step into my friend's living room and see a tall guy in a pale orange V-neck sweater, his long frame stretched out on her couch. He's not handsome in the conventional sense. He has more of a Donald Sutherland, character-actor look. He has a big Roman nose, shaggy brown hair, and the trusting blue eyes of a priest. When Mark gets up to shake my hand—a tall building unfolding itself—I feel a tug of attraction.

The restaurant we go to is loud and frenetic, with waiters zig-zagging this way and that, and a classic rock soundtrack booming. Fajitas sizzle on big cast iron trays, the spike of jalapeños and lager in the air. Mark and I sit at one end of a long table filled with other couples. During the entire three-hour dinner, we talk only to each other. We have to shout to hear each other.

"What's your favorite movie?" he asks loudly.

I take a sip of my white wine. Mark is drinking beer.

"*The Sting*," I say. He grins.

"I want to shake your hand," he says. "That's my favorite movie, too."

Oh, Jesus, I think. *Shake my hand? Really? So corny*. But I love how we're talking; everything is easy and natural. For once, I'm not planning what I'm going to say next. Being with him already feels like slipping into comfortable shoes, sailing into a safe harbor. Mark seems to like me. Right off the bat, I have a vague sense of having the upper hand—of being desired more than desiring. As we part ways in the dark on my friend's front porch, Mark kisses me.

"You do that very well," he says.

39

Jake never told me I was a good kisser.

He calls me the next day. That weekend, we go see *Silkwood*. Afterward, we slide into a scuffed wooden booth at the Broadway 50-50, a dive bar where I spent many a high school night getting plastered. Mark orders a second round of beers while I'm in the restroom. He didn't even ask if I wanted another—an encouraging sign! On our third date, we walk around the track at a high school near his duplex; we're trying to impress each other with feats of physical fitness. The tall chain-link fence is locked, and Mark hoists me easily over it, causing me to all but swoon internally. I love the dark fur on his forearms and the well-muscled calves on his long legs. After the walk, back at my apartment, I make a big plate of gooey nachos and pour pilsner into frosty glasses.

"You don't know this about me, but I'm kind of a pig," Mark says, pulling a strand of stringy cheese and stuffing it in his mouth. I think but don't say, *You don't know this about me:* I've *been intermittently overeating since high school.*

A few nights later, Mark makes dinner at his modest rental, situated in a neighborhood dotted with stray dogs and rusted-out cars. He's a talented but struggling stained-glass artist who works at a shop right across the street. He bustles around his forties-era kitchen, slicing cucumbers for salad and stirring a pot of red spaghetti sauce that bubbles on the stove. To my utter delight, he fills an oversized Pat O'Brien's Hurricane glass almost to the brim with Inglenook Chablis. It's a bargain-basement brand, sure, but frankly, volume is more important than taste to me.

"Here you go," he says, grinning.

We have sex that night. In the days ahead, as we repeat the act, there are no fireworks on my part (beyond the ones I fake). I finally come clean to Mark because he's so damn trustworthy (it's those priest-like eyes). I confess that I'd recently seen a sex therapist because I'd never been able to climax, either on my own or with a partner. After working with the therapist, an older woman with a cap of silver hair whose matter-of-fact approach to sex drained away my sense of shame, things had resolved, at least under my own auspices. Revealing this to Mark somehow releases the pressure, like air from a balloon. He knows I struggle, so I don't have to pretend, don't have to fake-pant like a porn star. Mark is a careful, generous lover, and in short order, wouldn't you know it, those fake fireworks become real.

A military brat who moved a lot as a child, Mark spent a big chunk of his twenties in New Orleans, where he did some hard partying and dabbled in drug dealing. Where Jake was constricting and tight, Mark is loose and generous—if not with his money (which he doesn't have much of) then with his desire to party and have a good time (again, *my type*). We go to Los Padrinos, a raucous, multi-roomed bar on the West Side, where we snort lines in the bathroom and cut loose on the dance floor. Driving to Port Aransas, I hold the automobile owner's manual between us as Mark snorts lines of meth off the cover. In New Orleans, we do prodigious amounts of coke and drive at high speeds in a Jeep across a bumpy field, our heads almost hitting the car ceiling. It's the highest I've ever been in my life. The next day at Mardi Gras, we take amyl nitrate poppers, so many that I end up with an excruciating headache. When I receive an expensive bottle of champagne as a Christmas gift from the oil company, Mark and I drink it on the balcony of my apartment, snorting lines of speed and eating Domino's pizza. We put down a blanket. I'm wearing a black lace teddy. We make love several times. *This is it*, I think. I've reached Nirvana.

Before we move on, a last word about my binge eating. One night, Mark and I are lying on the floor of my living room on a blanket, drifting off to sleep. The TV glows blue in the semi-darkness. We had spent the day at the lake. Suddenly, I remember having most of a cold roast chicken in the fridge. I want to eat it. Badly. I tell Mark he has to leave, I have an early-morning meeting. He harrumphs, gives me a wounded look, then slips out the door. I grab the plate of chicken and tear into it. The Monty Python skit on TV shows an enormously fat man gorging at a restaurant. In between courses, he projectile-vomits into a pail. The waiter gives him one final treat, a thin mint. He explodes in a Grand Guignol extravaganza of guts and gore.

I put the chicken leg down. I don't know if the skit worked some sort of aversion therapy magic on me, or if finally having a person in my life who loved me filled a hole in my psyche. After this night, I never binge again.

My assorted neuroses—sexual dysfunction, eating disorder, panic attacks—are dropping like wingless flies. However, the big one, the Grand Kahuna, the taproot of all my eventual troubles, will prove far more resistant.

One day, out of nowhere, Mark says that all the hard partying has to stop. We're hanging out in my apartment, an ordinary weekday, trying to decide what to have for dinner. A few rays of the dwindling evening sun cast parabolas of light through the glass balcony doors. Mark stares into my near-empty refrigerator, then resolutely shuts the door. He turns to me, discomfort pulling down the corners of his mouth. *Is he feeling sick?* He looks vaguely hemorrhoidal.

"Listen, I left New Orleans to get away from drugs," he says. "I don't want to repeat the same thing here."

Wait a minute, what? Where is this coming from? He likes to do drugs as much as I do. If this is a sudden courtroom trial, there are clearly two co-conspirators here.

I rise from the bar stool and come around into the kitchen. I lean back against the wall, fold my arms across my chest, and try to feign nonchalance. I'm feeling attacked, but I'll be damned if I'm going to let him pin this on me. I was hardly doing hard drugs anymore until he came into the picture.

"You've been wanting to do speed as much as I have."

"I know," Mark says. He unfolds my arms, grabs my hands, and holds them. His mouth slightly unfrowns itself.

"I'm not blaming you. I'm just saying we should stop. We don't need it."

I let go of his hands, roll my eyes, and throw my arms in the air. A gesture of surrender.

"Sure. I don't care. I can take it or leave it."

"Good."

"Good. Fine. No more drugs."

It's easy: I don't miss drugs at all. But a few weeks later, Mark and I have just finished eating dinner at his place. I wash the few dishes, hang the dish rag on the stove handle, and sit back down at the kitchen table. It's a battered rental table, with a ceramic pot of wilted African violets at its center. The air still holds the pungent aroma of the shrimp Mark fried, which we'd dipped in cocktail sauce. We've been dating several months, and Mark has already brought up the subject of marriage.

A half-full bottle of red wine rests between us. When I pick it up to refill my glass, I notice Mark watching.

"You drink a lot," he says.

I stop mid-pour and pull a mug of incredulity.

"What do you mean?" I set the bottle down.

"It just seems like you want to drink every night," Mark says.

The tiny seed pod of worry that has lain dormant in my mind—the one planted in San Marcos, Austin, and on a strobe-lit dancefloor in San Antonio—suddenly stirs, sprouting a shiny green leaf.

Mark is looking at me expectantly, as if this is a subject he's been chewing on for a while. It's not a topic I want to talk about *at all. What's happening to my fun party boy? Why is he throwing cold water all over the great scene we have going? Am I about to be duped with another case of false advertising?*

I square my shoulders, lift my chin up in the air.

"You like to drink, too. Isn't this sort of like the pot calling the kettle black?" I ask. Defensiveness drives me to cliché.

Mark runs his fingers along the edge of the plastic place mat, considering it.

"Maybe we both have a problem." Pause. "I don't want to drink every night, but I do because you do."

How much do I disclose? Do I tell Mark I've worried about my drinking in the past? That there have been a few, um, embarrassing incidents here and there? What if he tells me I need to stop drinking?

But how can I lie to a priest?

I slump over the table. Here it goes.

"I actually went to a 12-Step meeting once." My mouth forms a haggard smile, my shoulders droop. I'm a deflated Macy's Thanksgiving Day parade balloon, collapsed on the sidewalk.

Mark's eyes go wide. He seems truly shocked.

"Really?"

"It was pretty weird," I say. *Please, please, please* don't ask for details.

We sit quietly. I can almost hear the wheels in his head turning.

"Maybe we should just cool it for a while," Mark says. "Just stop. I'll go to a meeting with you."

"OK. Let's do it." I sit back in my chair, clasp my hands, and nod purposefully. This has turned out to be a terrible evening.

I don't want to go to another 12-Step meeting. But resisting might convince Mark I truly have a problem. I get up from the table and pour the rest of the wine down the chipped kitchen sink, watching forlornly as the purplish liquid circles the drain and disappears, the acidic bouquet floating up into my nostrils. Goodbye, my friend.

Two days later, we pull up to a Korean Christian church, an erstwhile regular Christian church that was sold when the surrounding neighborhood experienced White flight and went to seed. We park, then spend the next ten minutes roaming around the various church buildings until we find the appointed meeting space, a classroom in the back of the fellowship hall. It's a humid day, cirrus clouds floating high in the sky. A great day for sitting around my apartment pool drinking margaritas out of sweating glasses.

One wall of the classroom is made up entirely of windows: I gaze out onto the parking lot and wish I was anywhere else. The room has that stuffy, musty church smell I recall from my childhood. Bookshelves hold prayer books; posters with scripture written in Korean hang on the walls. A half-dozen bunch of jowly old men in golf shirts sit around a circular table, mugs of coffee in their hands. They smile up at us as we enter the room. Fresh prey.

"Well, hey there, strangers!" says one of the men, jumping up to shake our hands. "Haven't seen you here before! Are you newcomers?"

"Are we what?" I ask.

"Newcomers. Is this y'all's first ever 12-Step meeting?"

I haltingly explain that I'd been to a meeting once before, but it was the first time for Mark. That we're just a tad worried about our drinking. (*My drinking*, I think but don't say).

"Well, you're in the right place!" His jowls jiggle as if some low-voltage current of electricity powers him. "Get some coffee and pull up a chair."

We do as we're told. The coffee tastes bitter. I dump in more Coffee Mate. Now it tastes chalky. The old guy, who seems to be the leader, tells us that there are other groups around town that draw younger alcoholics. He's implicitly noting that we're younger by several decades than the other poor sops sitting around the table.

"These kids all end up being great friends," he says. "When they get together at each other's houses for barbecues, parties, whatnot, the gatherings usually turn into mini-meetings."

He smiles at me, as if what he just said was a good thing. I smile back, thinking, *I'd rather chew my arm off.*

As with my first 12-Step meeting, I tune out most of what gets said. Something about the importance of having a spiritual awakening to be released from the desire to drink. *Whatever.* Mark and I steal glances at each other. In the car going home, we're strangely silent.

"Well, that was interesting," he finally says.

I stare out the window. I'm afraid if I say anything negative, Mark will chalk it up to resistance.

"Kind of like the first one I went to. I think they're all pretty much the same."

For the next several days, our evenings move at a glacial pace, as if caught in a thick sludge. We watch TV, cook dinner. I watch the clock, its arms caught in the same mire, willing time to move faster so I can get in bed and go to sleep, escaping the relentless boredom that is being sober at night.

That weekend, Mark and I have dinner at a red-tablecloth Italian restaurant. We're celebrating: I just got hired at one of the two local newspapers in San Antonio. My mother, who had friends at the paper, told me about a job opening for a reporter. For months, I'd been writing freelance articles for the magazine of a local credit union where my older sister worked. I gathered up my crappy little cache of stories and applied for the job. I was scared, but Mark encouraged me; he knew I was miserable at the oil company and dreamed of becoming a writer.

I didn't get that job. But I was offered another: a low-paying, entry-level position filing paperwork and updating a list of things to do around town in the paper's entertainment section. It's not even close to a reporting job, but it puts me in proximity to reporters and editors. Maybe I can learn the rudiments of writing through osmosis. In any case, it gets me away from my irascible oil company boss.

Mark and I eat shrimp and sip iced tea. The air is thick with the smell of sizzling garlic and toasted bread, mingled with the communal buzz of human conviviality. But our celebration is a pretty glum affair. We stumble over our small talk. I could jump out of my skin. Only a few years before, Vanessa, her older brother, and I got smashed at this very restaurant. At one point, I glance around and notice: *every single diner is drinking wine—luscious goblets of red—except for the two-year-old at the next table, who keeps throwing his bread on the floor.* Yep, I've been relegated to toddler status.

After dinner, out in the parking lot, I slide the key into the door of my blue Toyota Tercel. I catch Mark looking at me over the roof of the car, a rogue twinkle in his eyes.

"To hell with it," he says. "Let's party."

How do I describe the sensation his words usher in? What had been wearisome black-and-white suddenly explodes into technicolor. We buy a big bottle of wine on the way home so the celebration can start in earnest. At age twenty-six, this has become the defining calculus of my life: alcohol plus evening equals happiness.

Anything less just wouldn't do. If you'd asked me why the world seemed drab at night unless well-saturated with wine, I would have stared at you dumbly and quickly walked away.

Chapter Six

Mark and I move in together, first into a derelict apartment near my work, then a two-bedroom rental in a low-rent neighborhood close to where I grew up. After a year, we get married. In addition to earning a master's degree in English at night school at UT San Antonio—a goal I undertook at the oil company to counter the soul-killing nature of my job—I've also become a full-fledged reporter. The osmosis worked, plus the mentorship of a talented editor who saw something in the nightclub and bar reviews I wrote on my own time *(oh, the irony!)* and promoted me to one of the two staff reporter positions at the Sunday magazine. Mark has reluctantly laid down his stained-glass tools for a job as a sales rep at a video rental company, so he can earn more money. We don't party as much anymore, but we drink almost every night, and always on the weekends. On Saturday mornings, we swallow Advil and consume greasy Mexican breakfasts to soak up the residual alcohol.

Here's a typical work night: we've just finished dinner. We're in the living room, getting ready to watch *Moonlighting*. Thunder rumbles in the distance. It's that exquisite moment before a storm hits, when the wind thrashes the trees in our front yard and tosses bright yellow leaves onto the front porch. The sky outside is half-light, half-dark; the damp smell of rain drifts through the screen door. Mark is on the couch, chatting with his mother on the phone. I'm stretched out on our beige carpet in front of the TV, ready for Cybil and Bruce. I have a stomach full of manicotti and Chardonnay.

Most weeknights, Mark and I put away a liter bottle with dinner. We have a little ritual: once the bottle is empty, Mark rolls it across the living room floor.

I'm supremely content. I take a mental snapshot of the moment: an ordinary Wednesday night in the first year of our marriage, with the rain coming down and the yellow leaves blowing, the wine bottle empty but I don't care because I'm perfectly happy and don't need a single thing.

We buy our first home, a modest three-bedroom with hardwood floors and a big backyard nestled in a cozy neighborhood peopled with other yuppies raising kids. We've been married about a year when my period is late, after months of our trying to conceive. The night before I'm to pee on the stick, we eat dinner at a Thai restaurant. With sore breasts and a full sensation in my pelvis, I have a sneaking suspicion I'm pregnant, so I only drink half my glass of wine. The next day, when the two little blue lines joyously appear, I make a vow: I will not drink while carrying this baby.

And I don't. It's not even hard. Something supremely important is under construction, a child I will protect and love with every particle of my being. My son (somehow, I know I'm having a boy from the very start) is going to have a different childhood than I did. No violent or absent father. No overstressed single mother wielding a brown belt. No fear. History will not repeat itself. I even quit my newspaper job to stay home.

In my fourth month of pregnancy, my cervix starts to open. My mother had taken a drug in the fifties when she began bleeding while pregnant with me. Doctors thought the drug, diethylstilbestrol, prevented miscarriage. What it actually did was cause cancer, deformed uteri, and other problems in the daughters of mothers who took it. Turns out I, a "DES daughter," have a congenitally weak cervix. My doctor stitches it shut and puts me on bed rest for the duration of my pregnancy.

At the surprise thirtieth birthday party that Mark and my older sister throw for me, guests greet and chat me up while I, huge with child, recline in a makeshift coffin that Mark built as a joke about my advancing age and to keep me off my feet, per the doctor's orders.

In my third trimester, I ask the doctor if I can have a single glass of champagne on New Year's Eve. Sure, he says. When the second hand ushers in 1988, the year our son will be born, Mark and I stand in the front yard, fireworks popping and fizzing around the neighborhood. It's a crisp night with a crescent moon. The starlight seems to pulse with the promise of a bright future. Under that starlit sky, we clink champagne flutes.

"I love you, Ba," Mark says, enfolding me in his arms. It's the pet name we have for each other.

"I love you too, Ba," I say.

"Only a few more months."

"A few more months."

*   *   *

Sam arrives pink and healthy, a perfect seven pounds, seven ounces, with a soft dusting of peach fuzz on his head. I had turned down the drugs they offered me at delivery, going *au naturale*. No chemicals were going to enter my baby's blood-stream!

We carefully squire him home the day after Easter, balloons fluttering outside the car window. My mother, who is dumbstruck with love at her first grandchild, brings over the leftovers from the family feast: baked ham, salad, mashed

50

potatoes, yeast rolls. Mark opens a bottle of white wine to celebrate. My grandmother tells me that a bottle of beer a day keeps your breast milk flowing, advice that sounds just right to me. I have one glass.

As the days pass, I'm exhausted but swoony in love with Sam, a physical yearning. I want to eat him. I kiss his tiny fingers, trace the curve of his shrimp-like ear. I even love the cake-batter smell of his baby shit. I stand over him in the middle of the night, change his diaper, the house silent around us. We're a club of two, safe in our cocoon of breast milk and Johnson's Baby Shampoo and daytime sleeping. I pick him up and place him at my breast, the rocking chair softly squeaking, and sing.

"I'm being followed by a moon shadow, mooooooon shadow, moon shadow."

When Mark walks through the door at the end of the day, I pass Sam off to him and make myself a whiskey sour. Just one. I take the drink, the kind my mother and I used to enjoy, and step into the steaming shower, letting the hot water stream over my sore nipples.

When Sam is about four months old, Mark and I decide to celebrate the Fourth of July with a backyard barbecue, complete with frozen margaritas. I love being a mother, but it's a lonely affair. All my sisters and girlfriends work, and Mark travels a good bit for his job. Having this little party feels like a reprieve. Mark moves around our well-worn kitchen, pouring a golden stream of Jose Cuervo into a blender, then some mixer, then handfuls of ice cubes. I slice some limes, their tart smell conjuring memories of our Caribbean honeymoon. I've been good, I tell myself. For the most part, I've had only one drink a day, worried that any more could seep into my breast milk. I deserve a little break. I look over at Sam, sitting in his automated crank-a-chair in the corner of the kitchen, the back-and-forth motion keeping him happy. The blender whirs, triggering an almost Pavlovian reaction in my body. Here comes alcohol!

"Are you sure it's OK for you to drink this?" Mark asks. He hasn't said a word about my whiskey sour habit. Now his brow is furrowed in concern. He tips the blender over my outstretched mason jar glass, the frothy lime-green slush dropping down in velvet folds.

"I'm only going to have two," I say. "Maybe three. Anyway, I have the breast pump. I can pump and dump."

We sit in the backyard at our weathered picnic table, Sam nestled on my lap. Mark mans the grill as clouds of mesquite smoke billow out of the barbecue pit each time he lifts the metal lid. Summer is in full leaf. The tall trees in our backyard cast a dappled green light over the lawn. The little old lady who lives next door is a master gardener; the scent from her magnolia trees floats over the fence. I rock gently as Sam gnaws on his little yellow ducky. The tequila flows through my veins. I haven't felt this good in a while.

"Ready for round two?" Mark says, holding up the pitcher. Beads of condensation glisten in the sun.

"Yes, sir."

I end up having four drinks, big ones. So does Mark. Maybe that's why he doesn't say anything when I exceed my stated limit of two. As dusk falls, I sit on the toilet in our bathroom, the breast pump going *wah-wah-wah* as it drains the tequila-tainted milk from my breast, a pale-cream liquid that I splash down the bathroom sink. Later, still sluggish from the drinks, I breastfeed Sam. As I lower him into his crib, a lazy thought occurs: *What if the dumped milk wasn't the polluted batch? What if some delayed metabolic action poisoned the milk he just swallowed?*

I push the thought away. In bed, I twist and flop, unable to fall asleep, the alcohol leaching from my blood. As it does, I grow more convinced that something terrible is happening to my baby. At midnight, I creep into Sam's room and feel his cheeks. They're warm and rosy, his small chest gently rising and falling. I stay awake the rest of the night, the digital clock marking my vigil, creeping into the nursery every half hour or so to touch his cheek, put my hand in front of his mouth. When dawn finally crawls across the backyard, shrubs slowly emerging from the retreating shadows, Sam wakes up, his gurgling self. Awash in relief, I gaze out his nursery window and think, *What sort of mother drugs her own child with possibly compromised breast milk?* But by mid-morning, the question has vaporized in the hustle-bustle of another day. Sam is fine. I'm fine. It was just a momentary lapse in judgment. Three months later, when I contracted a stomach virus, I used it as an excuse to stop nursing. In truth, I was tired of having to strictly limit my drinking.

I don't tell myself that, of course.

Chapter Seven

Whether it's the stress of having a new baby or the strain of having too little money, Mark and I start fighting. We bicker over stupid shit: how Mark leaves the contents emptied from his pockets all over the house, how I don't keep things as neat as I should, how Sam is getting too fat because I overfeed him. (He throws up sometimes, so I feed him again because I can't abide the thought of him being hungry.) We go see a cut-rate marriage counselor, the first of many over the years. We stop after several sessions—when her stabs at getting us to communicate start to feel ridiculous. Soon after, Mark gets promoted at the video company, a new position that brings in more money but entails even more travel.

Whenever Mark is out of town, I can drink as much as I want. Not that he's openly critical of my intake. I somehow know intuitively that when Mark is around, I have to stay within certain bounds. With him gone, I'm free, and it's in this freedom that I begin to see the first glittering edges of danger.

One afternoon when Mark is on the road, Sam and I have just returned from the grocery store. I'm unloading brown paper bags from the trunk of my car. He's swinging in his crank-a-chair in the living room, happy as a little Buddha. Thanks to a nearby gym that offers cheap classes and free babysitting, I'm in the best shape of my life, my arms ropy with sinew. I pop in and out of the house, setting the bags on the kitchen counter, looking forward to the approaching cocktail hour. On my last trip, I snuggle a bag holding a jar of applesauce and a cantaloupe on my hip; my other hand grasps the neck of a liter bottle of Chardonnay, my supply for two nights, maybe three. (Who am I kidding? Two at most.) As I bound up the top step, the bottle slips from my grip and shatters into a million pieces on our concrete front porch.

The wine makes soft splashing sounds as it trickles down the steps. I stare at the pile of shards. It seems like a test: *Do I need the wine so badly that I'm willing to buckle my son back into his car seat and make a return trip to the store? All for a bottle of wine?* This debate takes four, maybe five seconds. I don't like what it's telling me about myself. I buckle Sam back into his car seat.

Some days I'm eager for Sam, now an energetic toddler, to take his afternoon nap because I'm ragged from drinking too much the night before. One afternoon, I lay down next to Sam in his new big-boy bed, the house quiet and serene around us. His toys are strewn about—why pick them up when he will only scatter them again? I cuddle up close, inhale the delicious puppy-dog scent of his head, my favorite smell in the entire world. Before he drifts off to sleep, he says something that shocks me.

"You smell like sugar and cheese."

Is my son, my sweet, towheaded, rambunctious, firecracker of a son, detecting the vestiges of my drinking the night before? Isn't that what stale alcohol would smell like? *Sugar and cheese?* Another night, as I'm walking toward our bed after draining what was left of a liter bottle (I never start drinking until I've put Sam down for the night), my toe catches the corner of our bedroom rug. I stagger and all but fall into the bed. *That was weird*, I think. *I've never tripped and staggered before.*

Must be the rug. I blame it on the rug.

*   *   *

When Sam is around two, I get a part-time job teaching a freshman English course at a community college to put some dollars in our ever-shrinking coffers. After a couple of semesters, I quit when the department switches all part-time instructors to teaching remedial English. Now, I wait tables at an upscale restaurant in a fancy neighborhood, a rather inglorious position for a thirty-something former journalist. Mark has changed jobs too, fleeing an abusive alcoholic boss (we're everywhere!). Now, he works as a manager in the video rental department of a grocery store chain.

We both wear aprons to work.

Things have reached a nadir. We fight over money. We fight over sex. Mark is like a man-child, unwilling to step up and handle any household responsibilities. I'm a nag, a shrew, picking at him like a scab. What I had loved so much about him during our courtship—his spontaneity, his willingness to be goofy—now reads as simple immaturity.

Though we're constantly broke, we still find a way to buy alcohol, sometimes using our Exxon card to buy beer at the gas station.

Even with all the tension, though, Mark can still make me laugh. One rare night out, we eat dinner at a cheap Chinese restaurant and go see a vampire movie. When I walk back into the living room after putting Sam down, I find Mark splayed on the couch, his neck awash in blood—ketchup, actually.

"Oh my God!" I crumple to the floor, laughing.

I try to remember what it was I loved about Mark, those first golden years when I felt finally seen and understood by someone—when I had someone in my corner who would love me, no matter what. But too often our days are marred by tension, often followed by hours, even days, of frosty silence. I start seeing a therapist at the local university on an income sliding scale, a program that helps hone baby doctors still in their residency. I think I pay about five dollars a session. My therapist is a guy named Frank, tall and nerdy with owlish glasses. I fidget in my chair across from him, tell him my marriage is failing, that I'm unhappy. I give him the childhood 4-1-1: absent daddy, angry mommy. Even I'm becoming bored with my story. I dump a mixed grill of concerns on Frank, all of which at their core feature the same self-obsessed whine: *Why am I not good enough?*

A question I leave out: *Why do I drink so much?*

I work with Frank for several months, convince him I'm better (I'm not), and quit.

Mark and I start attending St. David's Episcopal Church, the congregation I grew up in, just so we can get Sam used to the nursery for the church's Mother's Day Out program. Neither Mark nor I are religious. He's a lapsed Catholic. I view organized religion as causing far more harm than help. We drop Sam off in the nursery, then go sit in the pews. At least the Episcopalians use real wine for communion. Soon, I befriend two other stay-at-home mothers who are members. They're Christian but not tight-asses about it. Joyce is dizzy and talkative, with long, folk-singer hair—and she's a hardcore liberal like me. Carol is tall and thin, with an East Texas twang, but harder to read politically. The most important thing: they both like to drink wine. The three of us start hanging out, sometimes drinking in the afternoons as our children play in the backyard.

To better fit in, I start attending a women's Bible study with them. We sit around a big table with a bunch of blue-haired old ladies and parse the Gospels. It's horrifically boring. If Jesus had something to say, why didn't he just say it instead of burying it inside a bunch of enigmatic agrarian parables? Mustard seeds, prodigal sons, shifting sands—

yawn. But Joyce and Carol are strong Christian women, so of course I want to be a strong Christian woman, too. When they invite me to a women's spiritual retreat at Camp Capers, the summer camp of my childhood, I eagerly sign up.

The weekend turns out to be a lot of singing and praying and sitting on hard chairs while an old priest yammers on about God. Again, yawn. But on the ride up, Joyce confides that when the day's spiritual exertions are done, everyone congregates in their cabins to drink wine. I'm looking forward to that part of the weekend. As the clock ticks toward ten on Friday night, I sit on my bottom bunk and wait for someone to break out a bottle. No one does. Bit by bit, my heart sinks. But suddenly here is Joyce, traipsing through our portico, empty Styrofoam cup in hand.

"Who's got the vino?" she sings. Suddenly, bottles emerge from overnight bags. I make sure to pace myself, to not drink more than the women circled around me. These church camp women don't drink fast enough—but I don't want to embarrass myself. One of my bunkmates is a young woman around my age. Slender and pretty, with a bob haircut. During a break on Saturday, as we stroll down an old railroad track, immersed in conversation, she suddenly says, "I'm a recovering alcoholic."

"You are?"

"Yeah. When I was a teenager, I came to this camp for a youth group retreat. One night, I stole the communion wine and got really drunk."

I look down at my feet as we walk. *Why is she telling me this? What am I supposed to say?* I give her a sideways smile.

"Did they catch you?"

"Of course. They figured it out." She smiles indulgently, as if forgiving her younger self.

My internal alcohol judge-o-meter nudges into gear. I, too, stole communion wine with another camper in my younger days, but I never got caught. I didn't get drunk. I kept my shit together. By my thirties, I've gotten handy at this form of mental gymnastics: comparing myself to "problem" women drinkers and deciding, *I'm not that bad.* It doesn't occur to me that normal drinkers don't have to do this. On the bluebonnet-strewn path, I draw a bright red line between myself and this young woman.

At dinner that night, as we stand in the cafeteria line, that same young woman overhears me tell someone next to me that I struggle with faith in God. She whirls around, eyes aflame, setting on me like a ravenous fly on a pungent cow patty.

"Have you accepted Jesus as your Lord and Savior?" she asks.

The question catches me off guard. *Have I* accepted Jesus as my Savior?

"Not officially, I guess." We inch forward in the line.

"Would you like to do it now?"

"You mean like right here?"

"Why not? Now's as good a time as any."

Part of me wants to tell her, *Hell no*, now is *not* as good a time as any. But another part is intrigued: What if this is the missing piece? What if publicly proclaiming Jesus as my Savior proves the cosmic key to unshackling my doubt?

"OK."

She takes my hands and pulls us out of the food line. Her hands are clammy. The aroma of fried chicken wafts around us, mixing with the low murmur of dinnertime chatter. Trays clatter against tables in the echoing food hall.

"Let's bow our heads," she says. We bow our heads.

"Dear Lord Jesus, I ask that you hear this woman right now as she pledges her belief in you. Please Lord Jesus, Father God, come into her heart right now as she opens it to you."

Through a slit in one eye, I can see women in the food line staring at us. *For fuck's sake, this is embarrassing. We must look like idiots.*

The young woman gives my hands a squeeze.

"It's your turn now," she says.

"Oh. Ok. Jesus, would you come into my heart?"

"I accept you as my Lord and Savior," she coaxes.

"I accept you as my Lord and Savior."

"Now and forever."

"Now and forever."

"In your precious name Jesus, we pray. Amen."

"Amen."

She lets go of my hands and pulls me into a tight embrace, her face lit up in a Joan-of-Arc fervor.

"You're saved now!"

I'm not sure what to say. What is the proper etiquette for being saved from eternal damnation?

"Um, *hooray!*" I hug her back. "Thanks!"

We rejoin the food line. I slide my tray down the silver rail, take the plate piled with chicken and carrot-raisin salad. I feel utterly the same. The prayer had altered nothing, all my doubts still snugly in place. Maybe salvation takes a while to work its way into your system, like antibiotics or Prozac?

That night, when Joyce steps into our cabin with her Styrofoam cup, I notice the young recovered alcoholic scowls down from her top bunk, then abruptly flops over like an angry fish, practically pressing her face against the wall. I make a mental note: *sobriety means you can't have any fun. It means pressing your face to the wall while the rest of the world parties.*

On the last day of the retreat, a traveling priest holds a healing service in the outdoor chapel. Word circulates that this guy speaks in tongues. The recovered alcoholic, who has apparently taken me on as a special project, urges me to attend with her.

"Come on, it will be interesting," she says, her eyes gleaming.

As we make our way across a grassy field toward the chapel, I gaze longingly back at Joyce and Carol, who sit at a picnic table with other women, drinking coffee. We enter the chapel, an open-air stone building surrounded by pasture, and take our place on a wooden bench toward the back. A soft wind blows through the sanctuary. The priest stands before the rustic altar. He's a middle-aged man with a buzz cut and wire-frame glasses, dressed in polyester slacks and a Sears Roebuck button-down shirt. He could be selling insurance. What was I expecting? Crimson robes? A crown of thorns? One by one, the women walk to the altar railing, where they kneel. The priest lays a hand on their heads. The instructions are to whisper your prayer request into the priest's ear before kneeling. I watch, mesmerized, as the priest holds one hand aloft, a stream of Latin-sounding gibberish flowing from his mouth. When it's finally my turn, I shuffle toward the altar, feeling trapped in a bad parody of a Flannery O'Connor short story.

"What is your prayer?" the priest asks.

"Help me in my relationship with my husband," I whisper.

A tiny hope flickers: Maybe this guy isn't a total nut job. Maybe his mumbo-jumbo really can fix my marriage. It needs it. Mark and I are fighting more than ever. We're adrift from each other, our son the only place (other than drinking) where our passion intersects. The priest's words flow over my head. When he finishes, I go back to my bench. At one point, while still speaking in tongues, the priest glances down at his watch, apparently not so slain in the spirit as to lose track of time.

The healing would prove as beneficial to my marriage as my faux conversion in the cafeteria food line. That is, not at all. But Mark and I continue to attend St. David's. The next year, we enroll Sam in preschool. I keep striving toward faith, a dog straining on its leash toward a bone that is forever being snatched away. Mark and I tell each other our church attendance is, if nothing else, a way to give Sam a spiritual foundation, even if he ultimately rebels against it like we did. Church is a great way to pretend-believe. All you have to do is sing, kneel, recite the liturgy, eat the wafer. Drink the wine.

One afternoon, not long after the retreat, Carol and I sit in the front seat of her minivan while Joyce is in the grocery store buying a six-pack of wine coolers. We puff on cigarettes, blowing the smoke out our half-rolled windows. My bare feet are propped up on the dashboard. I relish the illicitness of it all: three stay-at-home moms getting buzzed. Carol is talking about her mother, who lives in a small town in East Texas and struggles financially. Carol is banging on about what a burden she is, how Carol has her own family to worry about, including an increasingly moody husband. Now she must contend with her mother's problems as well.

"It doesn't help that she lives in *Nigger-ville*," Carol says, rolling her eyes.

I freeze mid-puff. Did she really just say that? Did this strong Christian woman, who sings songs of praise each Sunday to a great and loving God, just spit out a racist epithet? Coward that I am, I don't say anything, I just laugh nervously. But another plank in the structure I'm building against church, against a God who makes belief so hard, falls into place. *This woman is full of shit*, I think, flicking my cigarette butt out the window. *Maybe they're all full of shit. Maybe the whole enterprise is full of shit.*

*   *   *

One day, out of the blue, my old newspaper calls: Do I want my old job back? You bet I do. As much as I love being Sam's mother, I miss my identity as a working journalist. Thanks to our low-paying, apron-wearing jobs, we lost our house after falling months behind on our mortgage. Now, we're back to living in an apartment.

It's nice to put on pantyhose and heels, to sit down in front of a computer and construct a story, versus serving salads to crabby octogenarians. I feel a part of myself that had been in hibernation come winking back to life. There's nothing nicer than coming home after a long day in the journalism salt mines to a crisp glass of Chardonnay, or two, or three. I'm rarely hungover at work. Not many women in the early nineties get to reclaim their jobs after quitting to have a baby. Given this second chance, I do my best to shine.

"You're making me look like a genius," the editor who argued for my return tells me.

But less than a year later, the head editor calls us all into the main newsroom. A gruff, no-nonsense man with a head of tousled hair, he stands up on a chair, his countenance grim, and for good reason: the newspaper is *kaput*. We're all about to be out of jobs. The national media chain that owns our paper has purchased the competitor and has decided to keep that outlet's staff while letting its own employees go. A few lucky writers will transfer over, but no one should count on that.

I call Mark, tell him the news.

"Holy shit," he says. We've gotten out of the hole financially, but we're in no way flush.

Like most of the paper's employees, I leave early that day, go home, and tie one on. Because of legalistic red tape, it will take months for the paper to close. During that time, I end up being one of the fortunate ones. The media chain's paper in Houston offers me a job as a feature writer. I take it. We pack up the car, the cat, Sam's toys and head east on I-10. We find a nice rental home with a fireplace and back deck in a formerly affluent suburb of Houston. The night before I'm to start my new job, Mark and I get good and drunk on the deck.

Houston is a cosmopolitan metropolis, huge and crammed with traffic. It's fast-paced and polluted and home to a myriad of cultures and ethnicities. It's a different order of magnitude from slow-paced, sleepy San Antonio, which is largely bi-cultural (Hispanic and Anglo) and saddled with entrenched, intergenerational poverty. I grew up in a provincial hinterland; although, as we leave, my hometown is in the process of blossoming into a Chicano arts center and a funky-cool town that will draw people, especially younger ones, from far trendier locales, even pretentiously hip Austin.

I'm excited but trepidatious: The Houston Chronicle is a much bigger paper. The creeping fear I've always harbored—that I'm an imposter, an interloper—stands a greater chance of being exposed. On my first day at work, I'm exhausted and hungover. I smile my way through it. But I get into a groove, writing stories large and small in the mostly female department. A few of my co-workers like to party. These are the women I gravitate toward.

The temptation is to turn Houston into a footnote, a place where for eight years I flourish as a reporter and my drinking stays under the radar. But it's in H-town where I first notice I must drink a little more to attain my nightly euphoria. The scientific nomenclature of addiction has a term for this: *tolerance.* Some mornings I arrive at work tired—because alcohol is the enemy of sleep. Advil is fast becoming a nightly ritual, a preemptive strike against morning headaches. At work I sometimes take those online "Are You an Alcoholic?" tests, hunching over my computer so no one can see the screen. I peruse the questions: Have you ever felt guilt or remorse about your drinking? *Yes.* Have you ever tried to cut back? *Yes.* Do you get angry when someone comments on your drinking? *Well, yes, sort of. Mark sometimes brings it up. But isn't it all just a matter of degree?* My finger hovers above the keyboard. Doesn't *everyone* experience a little next morning embarrassment occasionally? Why would you need to cut back if you don't have a problem? Mark hasn't commented on my drinking in a while. I change all my answers to "No."

Here's a question they should consider adding to those tests: Do you find yourself repeatedly taking "Are You an Alcoholic" tests? *Yes.*

Sometimes, as I'm pouring a third glass of wine on a work night, a thought arises: *Why am I doing this?* I offhandedly mention this thought to a female co-worker, a woman who I know is in recovery from alcoholism. She looks at me with an arched eyebrow.

"Did you know that seven to ten percent of adults consume most of the alcohol in the US?"

I don't like her telling me this. I make a mental note to never mention my drinking habit to her again.

I'm now the main breadwinner. Mark works two, low-paying part-time jobs, as a Gatorade sales rep and a male nanny for kids in a nearby subdivision. He takes care of Sam, now in kindergarten, in the afternoons. We have more money, but there's still stress and bickering between us. One night, we're driving home from our favorite Italian restaurant. We've both had a few. We're arguing about some stupid thing, who knows what. Suddenly, Sam, in the backseat, bursts into tears.

"Stop fighting!"

It shuts us up. For the moment.

Mark says he's feeling rudderless, and into this vacant space walks an event that will mark a major turning point in my husband's life. It starts in the most pedestrian of ways. One day, while he and Sam are at a Houston mall, he reunites a lost toddler with her mother. The next day, it happens again at the same mall, this time with a young boy. That night, sitting on the couch, Mark tries to explain to me what happened after he returned the second child: a sort of out-of-body experience that for a handful of minutes made him feel cosmically connected, in fact, *in love*, with every other person in the mall. It sounds like crazy talk to me—perhaps a reaction to the antidepressants he keeps going on and off to deal with his intermittent bouts with depression? But Mark insists it was a genuine spiritual experience.

We don't know it this night, talking on the couch, but the short-lived episodes at the mall would end up guiding Mark's life in the decades to come, sending him to college for a human services degree and toward a career helping homeless and mentally ill people.

As for me, I have no use for God: wine is my spiritual experience. But my religion is starting to cause me a wee bit of trouble.

*   *   *

In the 12-Step world, people talk about "moments of clarity," little microbursts of truth that power through the permafrost of an alcoholic's denial. A brief window opens, letting the drinker see in stark relief how bad their problem truly is. The window can stay open, triggering recovery, or it can snap shut again. One such moment happens to me during track-and-field day at Sam's elementary school.

By now, Sam is in first grade, a smart, gregarious kid who has trouble sitting still. His white-blond hair is darkening, his baby fat has disappeared. He's hilarious and high-spirited, afraid of nothing—traits that I relish. So what if he's always speaking out and cracking jokes in class?

We've moved to Clear Lake, a "planned community" not far from Galveston, where we bought a home in a Norman Rockwell-esque neighborhood of one-story brick houses, community pools, and tidy lawns. We'd moved there mainly for the public elementary school, which my research had revealed as one of the best.

A lot of the other mothers are stay-at-home types, with engineer husbands who work at nearby NASA or oil companies in downtown Houston, thirty minutes away. In my goal to prove that I'm one of those working mothers who still finds time to be involved in my son's education, I volunteered to be one of the field monitors. The night before, I had over-imbibed with wine. So here I come to the grassy expanse behind Armand Bayou Elementary, feeling wan and tired but determined to put on a good performance.

"You were supposed to bring water!" Sam yells when I show him the cold bottle of Coke I've brought in an insulated box. "All the other moms brought water!"

My normally cheery son is angry, hands on his hips, his lower lip extended.

Panicked, I rush to the nearby convenience store and buy several bottles of water. The games have already begun when I return. The glaring sun has turned the slight twinge above my left eyebrow into a full-blown headache. The bottle of Advil is in my purse in my car. I forgot to bring my clip-on sunglasses. I take my appointed place on the field and do my duty, noting times on a clipboard. In between the runners, I glance around at the other mothers. Everyone looks so fresh and wholesome in their khaki Mom shorts and knit tops, shiny hair tied back in smooth ponytails. *Are any of them exhausted? Do any of them drink too much at night?* The proof seems as irrefutable as the clipboard I hold in my hand: I have a drinking problem. But that night, I go easy on the wine. The next day, I feel like a million bucks. Problem solved. Move along. Nothing to see here.

The window snaps shut.

Chapter Eight

Mark earns his degree at the nearby University of Houston–Clear Lake and enters the world of non-profit work. Our hyperactive son thrives, once we reluctantly put him on a small dose of Ritalin that allows him to focus in class. He's even placed in the gifted and talented program.

Sam makes friends with another fifth-grade boy whose parents live in one of the nearby, more upscale subdivisions. Scott and Janie are like us: they like to party. I figure this out one evening when I pick up Sam from their house. As I chat with Janie while Sam gets his backpack, I can smell alcohol and cigarette smoke wafting in from the living room. A few days later, I swim over to Scott at the community pool. I drop a few anecdotes about how Mark and I like to drink. As I swim away, I think: *Man, did I just come off like a total alcoholic?*

But it does the trick. Scott and Janie invite us over to their house for dinner. Soon, we're getting together regularly, mostly at their larger home a few blocks over, which has a swimming pool and hot tub. Janie, it turns out, also likes to smoke marijuana. After one of her sumptuous, wine-heavy feasts, we sit in their bubbling hot tub, soaking and taking tokes of a joint while Sam and their son and older daughter watch a video in the living room. It feels illicit, thrillingly subversive: a quartet of responsible parents getting baked on grass in suburbia. What would the gals in the PTA think? Scott, who is a bit of a gourmand, likes to sip his scotch and puff on one of his cigars as he cooks in the tub. Janie, after downing tequila shots and cooking an extravagant Mexican spread, can somehow still do backflips off her diving board. After our little weekend bacchanalias, Mark and I can just pour ourselves the few blocks home, Sam oblivious to our altered states.

What I notice about Scott and Janie, though, is that they always know *when* to put it down. Sometimes they have to tell Mark, no, he can't open another beer, it's time to wrap things up, they have things to do in the morning. At one particularly hedonistic get together, I goad Janie into doing a shot of Bushmills in the kitchen. It's already well past midnight.

The next morning, I call her, cratered by a hangover. *What were we thinking?*

"Well, you were the one who wanted to do the Bushmills." She's right. I was the one.

*   *   *

Something happens toward the end of our almost eight-year sojourn in Houston that upsets the apple cart of my happiness and changes everything.

I forget how to sleep.

Work pressure triggers it. I'm worried about a big assignment and whether I'd be able to pull it off by the deadline. I look at the digital clock. It's eleven. Eight hours before I have to wake up. *Go to sleep. Go to sleep now.* Midnight. Seven hours. *Should I get up and drink more wine? Would that be crazy?* Twelve-thirty. Finally, I feel myself begin to drop off, my limbs loosening into ooze. Just as I start to tumble down the velvet tunnel of sleep, a tiny corner of my consciousness hits a snag: what's left of my still-awake mind tells my going-to-sleep mind that I'm finally going under. This realization yanks the fabric right off the table, dishware crashing to the floor as I jolt back into consciousness, cortisol pumping through my veins. *Goddammit. Just stop it. Stop.* I stretch. Take a few deep breaths. Vow to not look at the digital clock, then look at it anyway. One-fifteen. I try silently counting, my old standby during youthful panic attacks, but my mind repeatedly returns to the fact I'm not sleeping. It's like trying to not think of a pink elephant. I silently repeat the Lord's Prayer over and over (true desperation). After a while, my body slides once more into ooze, my thoughts a random widening gyre. But once again, I hit the snag and am slammed back into the darkened room, the twisted sheets, my infernal pulsating consciousness.

The whole world is asleep except me. I'm so tired my bones ache. The clock reads three a.m. I beat my fists against my thigh. Sit on the toilet, hunched and naked, trickling pee as I curse myself. Back into bed. Slide. Ooze. Jolt. Slide. Ooze. Jolt. How many times does it happen? Five? Ten? At some point, my brain succumbs, and everything goes to black.

The next day at work, I slump at my desk, almost swaying from fatigue. My eyes keep wanting to close and I must force them to stay open. The newsroom hubbub all around me, phones ringing, people talking and laughing, only throws my weariness into starker relief. I am a gray shadow surrounded by a whirlwind of color and sound. I open the story and start typing, forcing my exhausted brain to focus. The fear that I won't be able to produce gives me a spurt of adrenalin. By noon, the story is almost done.

"Are you finished yet?" my editor asks, sidling up to my desk, her eyebrows lifted.

"Almost," I say with a wan smile, doing my best impersonation of how a rested person might act.

The story runs to rave reviews. But what if it's just a fluke? What if I can't count on adrenalin to pull me through? What if my inability to fall asleep ends up costing me my job? Will we lose our house? Will Sam end up in some horrible school?

The insomnia doesn't subside. It comes back night after night. Each day, as dusk descends, dread fills my body.

"I don't know what I'm going to do," I say to Mark one morning, my voice quavering. "I've got to be able to function."

"I don't know what to say, Ba," he says. "Just try to relax?" Mark has always been able to fall asleep within minutes.

"Relaxing is the problem," I say, hunched over the breakfast table. "I can't relax and let go and just fall asleep. My mind won't let me. If you've never experienced this, you won't understand."

Mark stares at me, his lips pushed to one side, his head cocked. I can tell he wants to be supportive, but this whole sleeplessness thing is getting on his nerves. He thinks I'm making a mountain out of a molehill. He thinks I'm being my usual neurotic self.

"Can't you just, I don't know, think about something pleasant?" he says.

I want to dump the sugar bowl on his head.

Every now and then, I catch a good night, causing hope to rush in that my ordeal is over. But it only sets me up for failure at the end of the day: *Will this night be as good as last night? Can I pull it off two nights in a row?* My insomnia begins to affect all facets of my life. My mood, my productivity at work, my ability to mother. In the car on the way home from picking up Sam from middle school, I explain that I can't do something for him because I'm too tired.

"I know, Mom," he says, staring vacantly out the passenger side window, backpack slung at his feet. "You're always too tired."

His words sting. The knowledge that insomnia is hurting my mothering only compounds the cycle, a devil's feedback loop. When I find myself in the kitchen at two a.m., chugging out of a bottle of Jim Beam (the booze relaxes me for about three minutes, then makes me have to pee, and then I'm wide awake again), I decide it's time to see a doctor. I perch on the papered examining table and try to explain what's going on.

"It's like this hamster wheel in my head," I say, worried the doctor will think I'm insane.

"You probably have a little OCD," she says, smiling at me benevolently. Her hands are folded calmly in her lap. She's obviously heard this complaint before. I'm nothing new to her. My shoulders lower some.

I picked this physician because her office is in a strip center close to my house. Her waiting room is so overcrowded that some people have to stand—I guess that was a warning sign.

"You're in luck," she said, rising from her stool. "There's a new drug that works great for people like you." She leaves the room, comes back in with her hands full of packaged drug samples.

"This is Ambien," she says. "You'll go to sleep right away and stay asleep; you won't experience any grogginess the next day."

"It's safe?"

She smiles benevolently again. "Very safe."

"Is it addictive?"

"No. Just take a break from it on the weekends."

I leave with a purse full of starter packs. It seems too good to be true: a safe chemical escape from the prison I've concocted for myself.

That night, I look at the tiny pill in my hand. Mark and I had consumed a bottle of wine at dinner at a restaurant. The sample package warns against combining the drug with alcohol. *I'll need to be careful*, I tell myself. But two and a half measly glasses of wine on top of a full meal surely can't be dangerous. I swallow the pill, climb into bed, and wait. I don't have to wait long. Within minutes, a silken curtain descends, shutting off the klieg light of my mind, smashing the *ooze-slide-jolt* cycle as if it were no more consequential than a buzzing gnat. It turns out that insomnia, that indomitable foe, is no match for the medicinal sledgehammer that is Ambien, a wily David that can slay a towering Goliath with a few well-placed molecules.

When I next open my eyes, my bedroom is ablaze with splendid morning sunlight. A chattering congress of birds outside my window celebrating the nine uninterrupted hours of sleep I'd achieved with no effort at all.

"I feel great!" I say, waltzing into the kitchen, where Mark stirs his coffee. "Ambien is amazing!"

Concern furrows his forehead.

"But how good is it that you're depending on a pill to sleep?"

I give him a level look. "How good is it to not sleep?" I quip. "The guy who wrecked the Exxon Valdez? He hadn't slept in days. Sleep-deprived driving is more dangerous than drunk driving."

After trying to go without Ambien on the weekend— when the *ooze-slide-jolt* returned with a vengeance—I decide the doctor is being overly cautious. If the drug is safe, surely there's no harm in taking it on the weekends, too?

I also discover that I can safely take Ambien even after getting drunk: it just gives me a case of double vision, a mild nuisance while watching *Saturday Night Live* before passing out.

But after time, unease sets in. Mark no longer hassles me about my nighttime chemical fix, but a thought chews at the back of my brain. *How healthy is this? How wise is it, really, to drug yourself into a stupor each night?*

I decide to get off Ambien. I try the various remedies developed for people with psychophysiological, or "learned," insomnia. I practice good "sleep hygiene." I practice "sleep restriction." I even go see a therapist, who tries to teach me a relaxation technique. Nothing works except my tiny little pill. My tiny little pill washed down with wine. I know that what I'm doing is unhealthy. I know that drugging and drinking myself into a stupefied sleep each night isn't cool. But the idea of giving up either the drug or the drink sends me into a panic. Even after I have sex with Mark one night and don't remember it, amnesia being one side effect of Ambien—I keep to my nightly dose.

Chapter Nine

My old newspaper in San Antonio calls me in Houston, asking: What can we do to get you back? My own column in the features section, I said. Done, they said. Come right away.

I'll learn later that the San Antonio editor was so avid to get me back because the Chronicle had recently hired away one of his favored writers. I was a revenge hire, essentially.

For the fifth time in Sam's young life, we uproot and move again. This is natural for Mark, whose father was a commander in the Coast Guard; he and his four siblings moved every three years. I spent all my formative years at the same address. But I'm more than willing to leave Houston, especially if it means I get to write a first-person column.

In later years, I'll wonder if our lives would have been different if we'd stayed in Houston. Would I have still become an alcoholic? Would our destinies have unfolded along a different track? It's useless to ponder. We pilot the car west on IH-10, the three of us moving inexorably toward our respective fates.

We buy a house in suburbia, a Brady Bunch-esque, split-level zoned for a high school with an affluent, homogeneously White student body. There's a large backyard with no trees, where the blaring sun prevents anything we plant from ever taking root. Our neighbors are all Republicans, judging from the political signs in their yards and the Hummers parked in their driveways. The floor of our house is done entirely in white tile, which will become the bane of my existence. I can never keep it clean.

Mark wanted to live somewhere funkier, but my fear that Sam might be in danger at an inner-city school with gangs, drugs, and violence—pick your stereotype—prevailed. As he enters his teens, Sam's safety remains my chief priority in life. I worry about him constantly. I'm a helicopter parent of the highest order.

The day we move in, I'm unpacking boxes in my spacious new kitchen that boasts a gleaming marble island and breakfast nook. I can't find the corkscrew. It's only a few minutes until five o'clock. The wine opener is not in the box marked "kitchen utensils." I look inside several other boxes. No corkscrew. Did we leave it in Houston? I start pawing through other boxes, my alarm rising. How will I explain to Mark that I have to make a special trip to the grocery store for a corkscrew? Finally, I spy the gleaming silver arms resting at the bottom of a box. I can breathe again.

At age forty-seven, I've attained everything I've ever wanted. A first-person column at a large metro daily. A husband who seems to love me. A happy son doing well in school. A nice home in the suburbs. But into this slice of middle-America paradise a snake will soon slither, the howling wind that just about blows my house down.

This is how it happens. For reasons that remain mysterious, I begin to lose my ability to hold my liquor. Addiction scientists would know, of course: my drinking problem is simply catching up with me.

The first time it happens, an old colleague of mine from Houston pays us a weekend visit. Her name is Barbara. She's garrulous and funny. Mark and I spend Saturday squiring her around to tourist sites. That night, we decide to eat al fresco on the back deck. Barbara helps me spread an animal-print bed sheet over the picnic table, lay down the plates, portion out the steak and baked potato. I'm hitting the wine pretty hard. As a light evening wind ruffles the bed sheet, I notice my words feel like small boulders on my tongue. It's an effort to get them out. I wonder if Mark or Barbara notice. I chalk up my difficulty in speaking to fatigue from our busy day.

The next night, we decide to order pizza and stay in to watch a movie. As I swallow the foam from my second beer, I realize I want another one. *Bad.* But it's Sunday night, the weekend is winding down. *What would Barbara and Mark think if I had a third?* Mark has not yet started monitoring my intake closely, but somehow I know on an intuitive level that getting a third beer would not be a good idea. So, I steal into the kitchen and quickly down the third bottle, peering around the corner to make sure Mark and our house guest are engrossed in the movie. As the last of the beer goes down, a painful gas bubble forms in my throat. I belch, covering my mouth so no one will hear. I stash the empty under the pizza carton in our trash can. This marks the first time in my drinking life that I hide an empty, a hallowed rite of passage among the problem drinking community. In 12-Step parlance, I'm a cucumber who has just officially turned into a pickle, and a pickle can't go back to being a cucumber, just as an alcoholic can't go back to being a normal drinker.

The next red flare goes off when we visit Sally, an old high school friend who teaches poetry at a large Midwestern university, over the Thanksgiving holiday. The first night, we eat dinner at a noisy steakhouse, sitting on wooden benches with groups of beer-drinking students all around us. I order a glass of red wine. Then another. It seems I can't get the wine down fast enough. Those small boulders in my mouth return. Perhaps I'm talking a bit loud.

"Stop drinking, Mom," Sam says from across the table, frowning. By now, he's a sophomore in high school, gangly and bespectacled, a straight-A student who still retains vestiges of his childhood physical affection for me. Sam has never been too embarrassed to hug his mother. He and I have always been close.

"Why? What's wrong?" I'm flippant, dismissive. I've had enough that his comment doesn't really ruffle me.

"Just stop."

Sam looks at his father, imploringly, asking with his eyes for him to intervene. But Mark is deep in conversation with Sally.

The next night is bitterly cold as we tromp through the town's main plaza, where crowds have gathered to kick off the Christmas season. Men dressed as Santa filter through the throng, handing out candy canes. On a makeshift stage in front of City Hall, a man puts on a puppet show. Fathers hoist toddlers on their shoulders. The Midwest wholesomeness is off the charts. After an hour or so, we decide a cocktail is in order. We prepare to duck into a toasty-looking bar, where steam frosts the windows and golden lights twinkle. But Sam balks at the doorway.

"I don't want to go in," he says. He scuffs his sneaker on the sidewalk.

"How come?" Sally asks. Mark and I trade looks.

Sam hesitates, jamming his hands in his jean pockets.

"I'm not old enough," he says.

"Don't be silly, Sam," I say impatiently. He's keeping me from my drink. "You're with adults. It's perfectly OK."

He reluctantly complies, scowling and not speaking as the three adults indulge in two rounds of martinis. Back at Sally's house, I tell her and Mark that Sam has recently made a few comments that my drinking makes him uncomfortable. We stand in her kitchen, a radiator hissing steam.

"I can't figure out why," I tell them. "Nothing's happened."

Sally and Mark look at each other and then back at me. It's important to me that they be puzzled.

"Maybe it's just him being a teenager," Sally ventures. Mark doesn't say anything, just pours himself a glass of water from the kitchen sink. "Yes, I think that's it," I respond. "You know teenagers."

Perhaps Sam's close bond with me enabled him to sense my unraveling well before Mark did. Or perhaps my husband didn't want to acknowledge what was happening before his very eyes.

If I could, I'd kick the Earth off its axis and spin it retrograde, *spin it and spin it and spin it* until I'm back standing in that Indiana kitchen on a cold November night. Only in this version of the past, the light bulb would spark on, and I'd realize Sam's concerns echoed the ones I'd sporadically entertained since my twenties. It would become clear to me that I was an alcoholic who needed to put the glass down and short-circuit all the pain that was to come.

But I'm stuck with the past I created, along with the guilt that will inhabit some corner of my soul until the day I die.

Chapter Ten

Not long after Thanksgiving, Mark and I start seeing yet another therapist for our continued bickering. For the first time, out of the blue, he brings up my drinking.

"She drinks every night," he tells the counselor, a young woman who looks like she's about fifteen. She's all wide-eyed interest, lapping up this tasty little morsel.

"You know, that's like pouring poison into your body," she says.

I blink at her. *Poison? What does she know?*

"I drink mostly on Thursday nights," I say, a bald-faced lie. "That's when *Seinfeld* comes on. It's must-see TV night."

The counselor says, "So that makes it a must-drink night?"

I smirk. Mark side-eyes me, a look that lets me know he knows I've just lied to a therapist. But he doesn't say anything, doesn't rat me out in front of her.

She sends us home with a packet of worksheets. As with our past therapists, we go through the paces with this young woman, practicing the same hackneyed communication skills. Then we drop out.

By this point, I'm a full-on Ambien junkie. Mornings are fine. I feel like my regular self. By late afternoon, withdrawal sets in, causing my jaw to clench and my shoulder to throb. At the grocery store, I want to ram my cart into fellow shoppers who move too slowly. I live for 10 p.m. when I can swallow my pill and swoon into blessed oblivion.

One evening, we are invited to dinner at the home of a couple we know from church. They have a magazine-worthy home on top of a cliff overlooking a river in the Texas Hill Country. It's a breezy midwinter evening, the cedar trees still green along the twisty rural road that leads to their house. As we drive, I clutch a bottle of red wine that is resting in my lap. This should be a relaxed, carefree evening spent with people we love. But I'm antsy, crawling out of my skin. I can't wait to down some of the red wine so that my Ambien-tightened coils will relax and I can behave like a normal person.

When we get there, the hostess takes the bottle of wine and places it far back on a kitchen counter. She is apparently serving her own beverage, to complement the meal she's made. It's something spicy, piquant. She's serving wine cut with Fresca. Cut a lot. It's citrusy and sour. There's no sweet warming, no glow in my gut. The whole night, I'm interruptive and manic, walking on sharp needles.

The hostess asks, "So, what are you working on at—"

"Oh, nothing important," I pipe, cutting her off. I launch into a mile-a-minute spiel about office politics at the newspaper. The couple stares at me, as if I've plopped on their couch from another planet.

On the drive home, Mark lets loose.

"You're addicted to this crap, and you have to get off it!" he yells.

"I know. But I have to sleep," I reply.

We huddle our heads, trying to find a way out. Mark has an idea. We recently joined a large, liberal downtown church, mostly as a way to get Sam into a youth group. One member is a doctor who is supposedly something of a pharmaceutical wizard. Maybe he can help? Embarrassed, I call and invite him to meet us for dinner at a Mexican restaurant.

On the designated night, mariachis strum oversized guitars and blow into horns while a woman with roses twined in her dark hair belts out *Volver*. We get there early, down a quick margarita and ask the waiter to get rid of the empty glasses. Rich walks in, a jaunty man who is a fitness buff. Over salsa and chips, I explain my little problem to the good doctor. He listens intently as I describe my history with insomnia, the troubles I'm having with Ambien, and my, *ahem,* drinking.

"Sometimes, I think I've been self-medicating all my adult life," I say, wide-eyed, hoping to impress him with my honesty. *Do I really believe this?*

"Your limbic system has gotten all messed up," Rich explains when I'm finished, making little circles around his ears with his forefingers. I will need to use another drug to get off the Ambien, and then slowly titrate down off the second one. Sounds like a plan!

This is how I'm introduced to Zyprexa, an antipsychotic with the helpful side effect of putting people to sleep. I'm to take a small, "subclinical" dose. Rich says I should abstain from alcohol for a while to get a clear picture of how the drug is working for me, and I should chart my progress in a journal.

The Zyprexa works. Miraculously. It's not a sledgehammer, like Ambien. More like a gentle lulling into sleep.

"I slept," I tell Mark in the kitchen one morning, my face creased from the sheets.

"That's great," he said, barely looking up from the paper. "I guess the doctor knew what he was doing."

I write one or two happy notes in the journal, and the not drinking? It lasts for about a week. Then I join Mark and one of his co-workers for dinner at a Mexican restaurant. He now runs a non-profit for people with serious mental illness. As they talk shop, I watch my spouse out of the corner of my eye as I tell the waitress I want a margarita, a specialty of this eatery, served ultra-strong in swimming-pool size goblets and adorned with an edible pink flower. He must be too embroiled in work conversation because he doesn't say a word when my drink arrives.

I get tipsier than usual on this one drink. My swallowing reflex seems blunted; I almost choke on a bite of cheese enchilada. An effect of the Zyprexa? I know people who take these types of drugs for mental illness aren't supposed to drink.

Several weeks pass, and I start packing on the pounds, another side effect of Zyprexa. It gives users a perennial case of the munchies. I don't give a damn. I'm sleeping.

I never call the doctor to talk about titrating off the Zyprexa. I thought, *Why mess with heaven?*

What I don't know is that Zyprexa, and other drugs like it, will play a role in turbo-charging the events of the next several years, damaging my relationship with the two most important people in my world: my husband and my son.

PART TWO

WHAT HAPPENED

Chapter Eleven

If I had to pinpoint the moment when my drinking finally coalesced into something my family could no longer ignore, something tangible and horrific, it would be Christmas 2005. But first, here's what alcoholism feels like: It feels like confetti.

You have a drink, then a second, and suddenly there's a fiesta going on in your head and body, a party that screams louder and louder: More confetti! *More confetti!* It's a floaty lightness-of-being, an outsized exhilaration that transforms an ordinary night into a Fourth of July fireworks show that spikes ever higher until the confetti God turns bleary and sleepy and the party is over. Until the next night.

Every problem drinker at some level understands that the confetti party is dangerous and damaging, whether in multiple areas of their life or just one. But researchers now know that physiological changes happen in the brain of substance-dependent people that make it exceedingly hard to take the party hat off for good.

Heavy drinkers who aren't alcoholics may decide, after experiencing some trouble, to cut back or stop on their own. It may be a challenge, but it's doable. For the *truly* alcohol-dependent however, it's not. Without help, it's impossible. The Big Book describes it as the *utter inability* to leave alcohol alone.

The confetti God must be obeyed.

It's a Saturday night, and Mark and I are trying to decide if we want to attend a holiday party given by a couple with whom we heavily party on a regular basis. (The wife, a stylish, put-together woman, likes to drink as much as I do. However, I've never heard her slur or seen her do anything remotely unladylike while blitzed.) We're both tired, especially me; the Zyprexa makes me fatigued by day's end. To Mark's great consternation, I've taken to passing out in my recliner before nine each night, the evening's quota of wine topped off by my magic pill. Before, he had a wife who couldn't sleep. Now he has one who seems to do nothing but. Some nights, Mark has to yell my name repeatedly before I rouse groggily from the chair and totter, semi-conscious, off to bed.

"You should be happy I'm sleeping without Ambien," I yell the morning after one of these incidents.

On this night, we decide to attend the party. I put on a long velveteen skirt with an elastic waistband, one of the few outfits that still fit. We drop Sam off down the block from the party, at a house whose owners have also been invited and have teen kids as well.

The couple's house is festooned with seasonal garlands, a gorgeous spruce twinkling in the corner. The spicy perfume of mulled wine beckons from the stove. I gorge myself at the table, shoveling in date bread, tortilla rounds, Swedish meatballs. In my other hand, I hold a large crystal goblet full of Cabernet. The husband, a jovial man and successful financial planner, ensures his guests' glasses are never close to empty.

"Top you off?" he asks, sloshing more wine into my goblet before I even say yes. Which, of course, I do.

There are about twenty people at the party—some friends from church, some strangers. The conversation swirling around me turns smeary. At some point, I make a vulgar joke in front of one of the male guests, saying he can grab my breasts. Things get blurrier. I slur and dominate every chit-chat circle I wade into. I find myself standing next to Daryl, a nice young gay man who is part of our regular dinner party circle. I like Daryl; he's one of the more restrained members of our group, a moderate drinker. In this room full of people, I reach down and grab Daryl's crotch. I do it twice. I wish I could describe his reaction, but it's lost. A little later, I stand in the middle of the living room and lift my shirt, exposing my ratty bra and cellulite-dimpled torso.

At some point we leave the party. Mark is drunk, too. It's rare for him to drink this much and even rarer for him to get behind the wheel so impaired. By this point in our drinking partnership, an imbalance has become clear: we drink together, sure, but Mark almost always stops before I do. Even though he's more than twice my size, he puts the glass down. I keep going, at least for another drink or two. Another difference: no matter how much he imbibes, Mark never shows the obvious signs of drunkenness that my son has started observing in me, the slurring and sloppiness that are driving him to worry.

Tonight, however, my husband will overshoot the mark.

We drive down the street and pick up Sam. It must be close to midnight, though I've lost all sense of time. Even in my drunkenness, I notice that Mark is weaving a little on the highway.

"Dad, you're not driving very well," Sam, fourteen, says from the backseat. He's pitched forward, his hands clutching the sides of his father's bucket seat. I'd describe the look on his face, but again, it's lost.

At home, I get out of the car and zigzag to the front door, stumbling on the grass slick with midnight dew.

"Oh my God," Sam says. "You're drunk."

"Isss OK," I say. "Isss Christmas. Everybody gets drunk."

The next morning when I open my eyes, a hazy simulacrum of the previous night's events swoops down, a kaleidoscope of horror. (A blackout would have been a mercy, but I haven't started having those yet.) *Did I really grab Daryl's crotch? Oh my God, I lifted up my shirt. Shit. Oh, shit. I stumbled and slurred in front of Sam.* When I walk into the living room, Mark and Sam are already seated on the couch, as if they've been waiting for me to wake up. I sit in a chair across from them. The air in the room is frosty, even with the heater on.

"We're both very worried about your drinking," Mark says, his mouth set in a grim line. There's a new, official tone in his voice. A steeliness in his stare.

Sam looks at me, the months of pent-up frustration shooting out of his eyes. Accusatory. Hurt.

I pull my fleece robe around me tighter. *Looks like I'm outnumbered here.* Normally, I'd start circling the wagons. But the memory of the night before is still fresh and raw in my mind.

"I know," I say. It comes out with a gust of breath. "I am, too. I have been for a while." Silence.

"OK," I say, with a finality I don't feel. "I will go to a 12-Step meeting. I'll stop."

I slap my knees with my hands, a gesture I hope telegraphs determination and grit. Mark nods. Sam looks at me with a hopefulness that breaks my heart. The three of us stand, hug. It feels good to have my son in my arms, but a corner of my mind rebels: *Mark was drunk too. He weaved on the highway. Why doesn't he have to go to a meeting?*

I would come to learn, of course, that Mark's occasional nights of overindulgence and my alcoholic drinking were two entirely different things.

But for now, a primal scream ricochets between my neural synapses: *I can't stop. I can't stop. I can't stop. Please don't make me stop.*

The next night, I drive downtown to pick Sam up from church youth group. I'm half an hour early, so I park and walk to a hotel bar across the street and order a sandwich and a glass of white wine automatically, a physical reflex. I sip it, the buttery liquid sliding down, and feel guilty, an emotion that is apparently now the mainstay of my life: *Will Sam be able to smell it on me?*

"You want another one, honey?" the waitress asks.

I say no, pay my bill. On the drive home, I decide to test this new territory between me and my son. Already I'm having second thoughts. *How am I supposed to live and not drink?*

"Was it really that bad, what I did last night?" I say, looking sideways at Sam. To my shock, he erupts into tears.

"Mom, *please* quit drinking!"

My son hasn't cried in years—because he hasn't had a reason to. Now he uses the back of his hand to rub the tears from his cheek, his breath hiccupping. Cold steel enters my gut.

"OK, OK," I say quietly. "I'll quit. I promise."

The next night, with every fiber of my being rebelling, I attend the third 12-Step meeting of my life. This one is held in an upstairs classroom of a church close to our home. I arrive early. I slouch in my car in the darkened parking lot, watch a group of smokers as they puff and chat near the entrance of the building, a swirl of white smoke encircling them. When they finally shuffle inside, I scuttle, crab-like, across the parking lot and dart inside. There's a bathroom next to the stairway that leads to the classroom. I push open the door, lock myself in a stall. I sit on the toilet for two or three minutes. *This is ridiculous*, I think. *Just get it over with.*

My heart pounding in my chest, I ascend the stairs and walk into the classroom. It's a big, brightly lit room, filled with thirty or forty people seated around a large table. Most are middle-aged. As I enter, all heads swivel toward me. There's no escaping now. An older man who seems to be in charge kicks things off with the Serenity Prayer—the courage to change the things I can, *yada yada* —and then asks, "Is anyone here for their first meeting?" Again, all heads rotate my way. I feel like a butterfly pinned to a board. I raise a tremulous hand.

"I've been to a meeting before, but it's been years. Over a decade."

"And what's your name?"

"Melissa."

"HI, MELISSA!" everyone in the room shouts in unison, a wall of sound that flattens my ears back.

I'd hoped to pass the meeting incognito, but it turns out I'm "the newcomer" and as such enjoy the dubious honor of being the most important person in the room. The attendees, all of whom seem to know each other well, direct their comments toward me, with seemingly interchangeable summations of how their lives were craptastic until they washed up on the sacred shores of recovery. I half-listen, dreading the moment when it's my turn to speak. Thankfully, the moment never comes.

One tiny message manages to worm its way through from the old guy who leads the meeting. During his brief oratory, his eyes are two shimmering dark orbs, burning straight into me.

"It doesn't matter if you're here tonight because someone else wants you to be here," he says. "Eventually, you have to want it for yourself."

Two people very much wanted me to be here tonight, and *that* I couldn't deny. Would I ever want to be here for myself? Highly doubtful.

After the meeting, people approach me and shake my hand. "Keep coming back," they say. "Don't leave before the miracle happens." "It works if you work it." One woman lingers. She is short, heavy-set, with what looks like a spray-on tan.

"I wanted to say something during the meeting, but I was too nervous," I say to her. "I don't know if I'm truly an alcoholic."

"So, what brought you here?" She seems marginally interested, probably wanting to climb in her Hyundai and get the hell home.

My father was an alcoholic, I say. Ah, she says. I give her a brief rundown of the Christmas party debacle. She nods her head. Ah. My son is worried about my drinking, I say. So is my husband. Ah, she says, again.

"Do you think I belong here?" I want her to say yes, unquestionably yes. Because I don't want to quit unless it's absolutely, one hundred percent clear that I must. I don't say this last part.

"What do you think?" she says. Her face betrays nothing.

I pause.

"I think I'm probably an alcoholic." She allows herself a slow rolling Cheshire cat grin.

I don't know it yet, but in the 12-Step fellowship, it's taboo to tell visitors on the fence about whether they're alcoholic what they should do. That's the bitch of it: alcoholism is the only disease that requires—*demands*—self-diagnosis. Probably because problem drinkers, as a group, are too rebellious to be forced or coerced into sobriety. Recovery, as they say, is an inside job, based on *attraction, not promotion.*

Here's the even bigger bitch of it: alcoholism is the only disease that tries to convince sufferers they don't have it.

The quick-and-dirty formal criteria, developed by doctors, is quite simple: addiction is the continued compulsive use of a substance despite negative consequences. It's a chronic, relapsing brain disease—a combination of physical, mental, emotional, and, in the 12-Step world, spiritual maladaptation.

It ain't rocket-science, folks.

It would take me years to grasp this fundamental idea.

After the meeting, I drive home, gripping the steering wheel, convinced my drinking days are over. *That's it. I'm done.*

But something curious happens over the next few days. I relive the Christmas party in my mind. Recalibrate the camera angles. Is grabbing a gay man's crotch *really* that bad? Wasn't it sort of funny? And don't lots of people get drunk at holiday parties? I start toting it all up:

And didn't that other woman lift up her blouse, mimicking me? I wonder if her family is making her go to meetings. Don't I have a good job? I've never had a DUI. I don't drink in the morning. My hands never shake. I've never had a blackout. The Big Book, which I've read, tells those in doubt about their alcoholism to go to a bar and try to stop at two drinks. Haven't I stopped at two drinks plenty of times?

I'm a defense attorney marshaling an air-tight case. What I don't know is that addiction specialists in recent years have done their own recalibrating, coming up with the medical nomenclature of *alcohol use disorder*, a condition that lies across a spectrum, from mild to moderate to severe. It tends to be progressive. But even the Big Book, written in 1939, way before brain scans and the advent of neuroscience, notes that some problem drinkers come into recovery before the starker symptoms manifest.

By the middle of the week, I'm the one asking Sam and Mark to sit on the couch.

"Look, I know it was a bad night," I begin in a sensible, let's-get-serious tone, splaying my hands in front of me, "But I really think I can control my drinking. Let me give it a try. I really haven't tried. Anyway, if I fail, I now know where the closest meeting is."

They're both silent. Sam glances at his father, taking his cue. He shouldn't have to be having this conversation.

"And Mark, you were plenty drunk, too." Maybe a touch of triumphalism in my voice. There it was, my trump card, flung on the table. Sam looks unconvinced, but he knows he's outgunned.

"If you think so," Sam says, a sadness in his eyes.

"Alright," Mark says. "Give it a try."

With those words, my world once again explodes into technicolor glory. I've slipped out from under the noose! Later in the kitchen, I swear to Mark I will only have two drinks a night during the week. "Two regular-sized glasses," he says, "not those huge Viking-sized goblets you pour."

"I don't pour huge goblets," I protest.

"Yes, you do."

"No, I don't."

"Especially with all that medicine you take, two is probably too much," he says.

"No, it's not. I don't take that much medicine," I argue.

"Yes, you do," he insists.

"No, I don't," I retort.

How many days later is it—a handful? Two weeks? I sneak a third glass. It's an ordinary weeknight, but I tell myself I deserve a third glass. The truth is, limiting myself to just two drinks has become unbearably hard. The confetti God starts tapping on my shoulder around three or four in the afternoon. By five, he's yelling in my ear. Every cell in my body cries out for liquid relief. It's a restlessness, a tightness, an unbearable thirst that cannot be assuaged any other way.

I pour the third drink while Mark is upstairs in the loft, then hide the wineglass on the ground next to my recliner, taking furtive sips as I watch TV. He must see me, because he flies like Batman down the stairs, straight over to my chair. He dramatically leans over me, bulls-eyeing the drink. I smirk up at him. Mark doesn't say anything, just scowls at me. I finish the glass but don't enjoy it. Mark now has a failure he can hold over my head.

Not long after, another incident happens. That's how I begin to think of them. My "incidents."

It could be weeks or months. The timeline is jumbled in my mind. I'm stealing sips of cold vodka out of the freezer on an ordinary weeknight, watching TV with Mark and Sam, striving to stay on the right side of the slur zone. When Mark asks what I'm drinking, I say ice water. I'm drunk enough to carelessly toss the empty vodka bottle in the garbage, instead of burying it carefully under the trash. The next morning, hungover, I sit in my car in the parking lot of a church. I'm about to go conduct an interview for a "clergy couple" story I'm working on. My cell phone rings. It's Mark. He found the vodka bottle.

"What the fuck! Now you're lying straight out to me, and you're drinking *straight vodka*? Really?"

My brain scrambles to come up with some excuse, some rationale, but he's caught me red-handed. The hangover doesn't help matters. I fold.

"I'm sorry."

"What do you mean you're sorry? You told me you were drinking water." The cell phone practically vibrates in my hand, so volcanic is his anger. Our roles are cementing into place: Mark is the grand inquisitor, I'm the infidel on the rack.

"I don't know why I did that. I'm sorry." I'm all but whimpering.

We hang up—or rather, Mark hangs up on me. I go into the church and interview the couple, feigning interest but barely able to follow their stories. Thank God for tape recorders. I know Mark is going to tell me I must quit drinking again. But then the oddest thing happens. He calls me later and offers an apology.

"Look, you just can't lie to me about your drinking. That's what I'm upset about."

By now, Mark has started going to the 12-Step program for the loved ones of alcoholics. But his commitment wavers. He goes for a time, then stops. Then starts up again. In this way, his pattern mimics my own stop-and-start dabbling with recovery. He doesn't quite get the concept of "detaching with love." In the wake of one of my incidents, he turns into the wine Gestapo, monitoring levels in the bottles nestled in the side door of the fridge, carping when I pour another glass. When he wants to drink, it all goes out the window. He's topping off my glass as we sit on the deck, laughing at my drunken jokes.

I take that as permission in the disturbed chess match our marriage has become.

Wouldn't you?

Chapter Twelve

How many incidents are there? Ten? Twenty? I won't pull you through the mud of every drunken episode over the half-decade. Let's stick to the half-dozen ones that involved Sam, as that's where the main hurt lies.

It's another Christmas. Mark and I attend a party at a couple's luxury condo overlooking the San Antonio River Walk, a shallow, greenish waterway that winds through downtown. First, we stop at a bar across the street for a martini. Then, we go to the party. I try and pace myself. Afterwards, we return to the bar with another couple. I have more martinis. How many? I don't know. On the way back home, Mark buys a six-pack, I lobby hard for it. I drink a beer on the ride back.

"You want one?" I ask Mark, rapidly approaching the slur zone.

"No, I'm done for the night." No judgment, just a simple statement of fact.

Once home, I pour myself into my recliner, my limbs jellified. Mark stretches out on the couch. We're watching TV. Sam walks into the room. He must be a junior in high school by now. A budding poet, he's holding a set of lyrics he's written that he wants to show me.

"*Whass that?*" I slur.

Sam turns on his heel and marches back to his room. Mark looks over at me after overhearing the exchange.

"Not a good idea, trying to talk." He seems more amused than mad.

The next day, the now familiar scene plays out: "I'm sorry. I'll stop. I'll go to meetings." I cry, but this time I notice a new skepticism clouding Sam's face.

Back I go to the same church classroom, only this time I don't need to lock myself in the stall. The look on Sam's face has re-galvanized my determination. Before this fourth attempt at the program, I make an appointment with my doctor after reading about drugs that help people stop drinking. My physician peers at me from his stool, an amiable man with a tight perm who I've seen for years but have never confided in about my alcohol-related concerns.

"Have you tried to cut down?" he asks.

I chuckle. Oh yes, I've tried to cut down. Not working. My doctor flips out his pad and writes a prescription for Naltrexone, a drug that's supposed to reduce cravings. It also negates the effects of any alcohol you do drink. I begin taking it on New Year's Day, once again staring down at a tiny pill in my hand, hoping for chemical salvation. The pill doesn't make me feel anything at all. I still want to drink. But my resolve pushes me to a new frontier in my adventures in sobriety. So, I decide to get a sponsor.

The woman I have in mind is elegant and witty, always dressed well with a sporty flair. I recognize her from one of my mother's women's advocacy events years before. When I first spy her at a meeting, my mind is duly blown: never would I have figured this woman for a drunk. If someone this put-together can be an alcoholic, maybe I am one after all. I sidle up to her after a meeting. She recognizes me as my mother's daughter.

"Will you be my sponsor?" I've steeled myself for a rejection.

"Of course," she says with a broad smile. Up close, her only imperfection is a slight whisper of acne scars along her jaw line. My new sponsor's name is Michelle.

"Have you read the Big Book?" she asks.

My goal is to score as many points with her as I can.

"Yes! All the way through."

"Great. There's a workbook I want you to get from the bookstore at Club 12. Fill in the questions in the first chapter, and we'll start working on the steps together."

"Will do, sponsor!" We chat on our way down the stairs. Standing at my car, she places a light hand on my shoulder.

"I want you to call me every day, just to check in," she says. "Even if the phone feels like it weighs a thousand pounds, we need to get in the habit of talking."

Fuck, this woman is serious.

I buy the workbook and fill it out. *Do I lie about my drinking?* I think of the times I've told Mark I've only had two drinks, the surreptitious swigs of vodka, etc. Sitting in a lawn chair under a sliver of shade afforded by an awning in our backyard, I mark "Yes." It's sweltering, the sun a diabolical globe in the sky. Sweat drips down my sides. I take a drag on my cigarette, hold the smoke in my lungs, repeat out loud as I exhale: *I'm an alcoholic, I'm an alcoholic, I'm an alcoholic.* Do you ever feel guilt over your drinking? That's an easy one. Negative consequences? Family conflict over your drinking? Yes, yes, and yes.

I've hit an updraft of honesty.

Michelle and I have our first sit-down session at Club 12. The large room that used to hold meetings is now the fellowship area, with long tables set side-by-side and an elevated area with a podium. The oniony smell of cheeseburgers emanates from the snack bar. Two oversized, black-and-white photos of Bill Wilson and Dr. Bob—the co-founders of the fellowship— stare down from the wall behind the podium, lending the room a vaguely Soviet Era feel. Michelle tells me a bit of her story, how she was a bad drunk from the very beginning, losing jobs, blacking out, and so on. It's the classic hardcore recovery tale. Already a tiny crop of doubt rises in my mind: Her story is not my story. (In 12-Step-speak, this is called *listening for the differences instead of the similarities*.) But I tuck my doubt away and spill about my past attempts to get sober. Including my struggle to identify as an alcoholic. How can I be powerless over alcohol when I can sometimes stop at two? How can my life be unmanageable when I haven't lost my job or my family, never been arrested? Sure, my husband and son want me to stop, but perhaps they're just overreacting. Michelle peers over her cat-eye glasses, an elementary school principal apprising a stumbling young truant.

She sits there for a moment or two.

"Do you have a strong desire to drink?" she asks.

That's an easy one.

"Yes, toward the end of the day. I mean, at night. Every night. I have to drink."

Michelle rests her chin in one hand and purses her lips. I get the sense she's performing. She's done this before.

"Sounds like an obsession to me."

Two older men pass by our table. Michelle gives them a glowing smile, which they return. She turns back to me.

"Do you experience a physical craving to drink more once you've had a drink? The Big Book calls it an allergy." She's talking about the confetti God.

"Yes."

"Do you continue to drink even though it's causing you problems in your life?" (Ah, the quick-and-dirty!)

"Yes."

Michelle's eyes flash with a gleam of victory. "Well, all that is the very definition of powerlessness and unmanageability."

I squirm in my chair, feeling nailed. This is what I've wanted, someone telling me beyond a shadow of a doubt I'm an alcoholic. But it's not the relief I imagined. Michelle's eyes are a tractor beam, drawing my gaze deep into hers.

"Girlfriend, you may not think you're an alcoholic, but you sure sound like one to me," she says.

But really—what makes her the expert?

"I know you're right, but at the same time, I don't know it. You know what I mean?"

Michelle picks a piece of lint off her sweater.

"Maybe you need to try some more controlled drinking."

"I don't really want to do that."

That's exactly what I want to do.

Michelle wants me to enroll in a substance abuse intensive outpatient program, or IOP, at a local residential treatment center. To learn more about my disease, she says. The next day, I learn the program is covered by my insurance. (*Will my bosses find out?*) The program meets several nights a week for four weeks. It's a major commitment, but I want to please Michelle. So, I drive to the center one day after work. During intake, the young man filling out the forms asks me questions: Do I have thoughts of suicide? Nope. Physical withdrawal when I stop drinking? Nope. Depression? Nope. Morning drinking? Nope. How much do you drink? Usually, two to three glasses a night, I say, leaving out the extra glasses I might sneak on the sly.

I tend to drink more on the weekends, I say.

"So, what are you doing here?" the young man asks jokingly. "What do you mean?"

"Most folks who end up here have more problems," he says, scribbling on the worksheet, not realizing the weapon he's just handed me. For now, I store it in my back pocket: an expert just told me I should have more problems if I'm truly an alcoholic.

Chapter Thirteen

The outpatient program is squirreled away in a small room deep within a warren of low-slung, red brick buildings interspersed with frond-dotted courtyards. The facility doubles as both a psychiatric hospital, complete with locked wards, and a residential drug treatment center. Each weeknight after work, I deposit my cell phone at the front desk—a rule to prevent junkies from calling their dealers for surreptitious dope drops. I walk down the shaded promenade, passing groups of dazed-looking patients who trudge from one building to another, under the watchful gaze of staff members. The outpatient class is small, a half-dozen people sprawled or slumped in couches and chairs drawn into a circle. Most attendees are young men, some with bluish tattoos. The teacher is a tall woman with an elongated neck who reminds me of a giraffe. A recovering alcoholic, she's fond, I'll soon learn, of telling the same stories over and over, such as the time a dentist tried to give her "a big 'ole bottle of Vicodin" after a root canal, even though she'd told him she was an addict.

"We have to be vigilant, y'all," she drawls.

We go around the circle and share condensed versions of our addiction stories. Most of the young men are enthralled by meth, crack, or prescription opiates. There's one other female, a brisk woman in her twenties who teaches grade school. Sometimes, she sneaks vodka into her classroom in a can of Diet Coke. (Geez, I've never done anything like *that.*) That first night, as several of us huddle in the breezeway and smoke during the break, a cold wind whipping our clothes, I confess I struggle with the idea that I'm truly a drunk.

"Really?" one of the young guys says with a sardonic grin. "You're taking Naltrexone, and you don't think you're an alcoholic?"

Over the weeks, I slip into a groove, sailing down the highway each evening after work, pulling up to the red brick complex, taking my place on the fake-leather couch. As time passes, tiny cracks appear in the armor of my denial. The first time it happens, we're watching a video. An aging priest is banging on about the evils of addiction, shouting in a hoarse voice from behind a podium. It's all standard 12-Step boilerplate until he says one thing: it's not how much you drink that makes you an alcoholic; it's the bad things that happen in your life when you do. I flatten back on the couch. In two sentences, the priest has obliterated one of the redoubts of my denial: that I can't be an alcoholic because my intake is nowhere near what I hear bandied about in meetings, where folks practically brag about their prior fifth-of-vodka-a-day habits or ability to polish off a case of beer in one sitting.

So much for that rationalization. If the priest is to be believed.

The second crack comes when the giraffe lady is writing on the chalkboard. For alcoholics and addicts, she says, their substance of choice at first brings them nothing but joy. On the board, she writes, "Joy and pleasure." Once the addiction process is underway, those good feelings turn into something else. She writes, "Shame and embarrassment."

There it was, bold and graphic in white chalk—the two bookends of my drinking.

Clarity is coming on hard. *I'm an alcoholic.* It feels like jubilation mixed with great lung gusts of relief. After class one night, I eat a roast beef sandwich at the kitchen island and listen as Mark and Sam talk about their day. I feel clean and light. Redeemed. Hollowed out. I almost glow. I think, *this is what it feels like to not live a double life.*

One night, the teacher calls me into her office during a break. Part of the program involves random breathalyzer testing. Tonight, it's my turn. I'm more than happy to oblige—no alcohol for this girl! I sit across from her and blow into the contraption, eager as a first grader. I've recently joined Weight Watchers and have started losing the pounds brought on by the Zyprexa. I've turned a corner. I'm firing on all cylinders. My sponsor is thrilled by my progress.

And then, things start to fall apart.

*   *   *

We're invited to a dinner party at the home where the Christmas disaster took place. It's a regular supper club we started a year or so earlier, a gathering of gay and straight couples alike. By this point, Daryl has forgiven me. As always, the wine flows. When we get there, everybody is in the kitchen, holding glasses of Merlot.

"I have an announcement," I say, deciding to head things off at the pass. Conversation stops. All heads turn toward me.

"I've quit drinking." I hoist a bottle of cranberry juice into the air.

"Really," says Howard. "Interesting."

Dead silence for a beat or two. Then the party swings back into gear, no one querying further about my noble undertaking. The jubilation I've been riding for the past few weeks suddenly tilts, wobbles, and crashes to the ground. At dinner, Mark sits at one end of the long table. I'm seated at the opposite end, next to a lesbian couple who are extremely nice but kind of boring. Like Daryl, they're moderate drinkers.

The table is crowded with plates of osso bucco, crusts of bread, and a battalion of wine glasses filled at various levels. I watch Mark as he drinks a second glass, then third (I'm keeping count). He's getting louder and sillier by the minute. As the bread pudding is being served, he accidentally breaks the stem on a wine glass, causing tidal waves of laughter. Instead of cutting him off, our host produces another goblet, fills it nearly to the brim. I talk little during the meal, trying to focus on my food. *Is that a hint of brandy in the pudding sauce?* I try not to notice the rising drunkenness around me.

After dinner, we gather in the den to take a group photo. Everyone is languid and loose, suffused with that soused dinner party glow, guffawing at jokes that aren't even funny. I am coiled as tight as a rattlesnake, ready to strike. But I force a smile on my face. *Let's get this over with, goddammit.* Our host sets up an automatic camera so he can be in the picture, too. He dashes toward the group before the flash goes off.

"Do a triple *salchow*," someone quips.

Monica, one of the lesbians, places a gentle hand on the small of my back as the camera snaps. For a moment, I picture sinking my incisors into the flesh of her palm, ripping the tendons of her wrist until bright red blood squirts all over our host's excellent Berber carpeting.

We're not out the door two seconds when I lay into Mark.

"This is bullshit. I'm not doing it again," I protest, stomping down the sidewalk toward our car. Night bugs chirp around us. The dark street is aglow with streetlamps. The house behind is still lit up and warm.

"What are you talking about?" says Mark, a container of bread pudding in his hand. His voice is all laissez-faire, all relaxed, as if he can't imagine there could be a single problem with this marvelous night. Of course, that only enrages me further.

"Everyone getting drunk. This is just not fair to me." I realize I sound like a spoiled toddler, but I can't stop myself.

"Oh, deal with it." He jams the key into the door, glowers at me over the top of the car.

"Fuck you. Can you even drive?" I'm practically hyperventilating.

"I'm fine. I stopped drinking over an hour ago." He starts the engine, looks over at me.

"You're going to have to get used to not drinking when others do, including me."

There's not an iota of sympathy in his voice. Not a shred of humanity or acknowledgement that this might be hard for me. I seethe, all but levitating off the car seat. I'm incandescent with anger. I want to shake him and shake him and shake him. I bang my hand on the dashboard instead.

"Why do I have to get used to it? Why can't you support me—since I've stopped drinking for *you*?"

Because that's what I've done. I've stopped drinking for Mark, for my marriage. Not for myself.

"That's bullshit. I'm not talking to you right now." He turns to the front, pushes on the accelerator. Clearly this conversation is over.

"Fine." I cross my arms and legs, a supremely pissed-off pretzel.

We drive home in stony silence. We don't talk much the next day. I smolder.

At IOP class, I listen as the crackheads babble on about squatting in houses with no lights, heat, or water. With hangdog grins, they recount adventures in burglary, theft, and sex for money. A couple of new folks have joined, adding their own tales of degradation to the mix: blackouts, mug shots, stern judges, and morning puking. *What the hell am I doing with these people?*

One night, the teacher confides that the staff, knowing I was a reporter, initially feared I was doing an undercover exposé of outpatient treatment centers.

"You didn't present the way most people do when they come in here," she says.

"Are you saying I don't belong here?" She doesn't answer, just smiles.

Not long after, I arrive at a conclusion: I'm most definitely *not an alcoholic*, and I'm most definitely *drinking again*. Just as soon as this infernal class is over. If I don't successfully graduate, my insurance won't cover it.

Toward the end of the class, one session focuses on "rock bottoms." It's a strangely jolly evening, given the bleak topic, with lots of relieved laughter. I'm feeling so secure that I decide to share one of my own stories. We were at Port Aransas with Scott and Janie, that couple from Houston. I get really drunk the first night. The next morning, on the beach, I uncharacteristically need to vomit but can't make it to the Port-A-Potty in time. I kneel behind one of our cars and puke into the sand, bits of sick splashing up on my knees, adhering to my sun block. Mark and the couple are in the waves as this is happening. As I'm retching, two cute guys walk by and glance in my direction.

"That was you?" one of the crack heads quips. Everyone breaks out laughing.

A part of the story I don't tell: The next morning, we picked Sam up from the bus station in Corpus Christi. He'd been at summer camp. That night, I get drunk again, slurring as we walk as a group along the beach, the stars twinkling in the sky.

"Sam is noticing you're drunk," Mark says, whispering so the other couple won't hear us. "You need to stop drinking."

I have a plastic cup of wine in my hand, sloshing some of it on the sand as I trudge by the edge of the waves. I scowl at my husband. *I'm fine, what is he talking about?*

Sam is quiet the next morning. On the drive home, he musters the courage to say something.

"You were drunk last night, Mom," he says from the backseat.

I turn around, look him square in the eye. His face is pale, drawn.

"I had a little to drink, but it was no big deal. Everyone drinks at the coast. Right, Mark?"

When we stop for a bathroom break, Mark is livid. While Sam is in the gas station, he turns and yells at me. "You can lie to Sam all you want about your drinking, but don't you dare try to pull me into it."

I'm sullen all the way home. That night, we go to a Mexican restaurant. When it's time to order drinks, I order a Corona—and a glass of tea, just to show I can balance it out. Sam watches me as I talk to the waiter, wrapped in the tense silence that is seeping into our home.

One night, the IOP teacher is out sick, replaced by a guy who is one of those blunt-talking straight-shooters that predominate in recovery circles. He's big and bulky as a bear; he doesn't smile, not once, for the duration of the class. I've stopped taking the Naltrexone, in advance of the drink I plan to have as soon as I finish outpatient treatment. Since this new guy is just temporary, I decide to venture into a little honesty. *What could it hurt?* I carefully say I'm having problems with the First Step, admitting I'm powerless over alcohol. My life really wasn't that bad when I was drinking, just an occasionally ticked-off husband. The guy listens as I ramble.

"See what she's doing?" he says to the group when I'm finished, with a little moue of self-satisfaction. "She's still playing that game between her ears."

I'm offended. More to the point, I feel found out. The guy writes in my file: 'relapse risk.' When our teacher returns, she calls me into her office. I figure I am going to be reprimanded, maybe even kicked out of the program. But she just laughs a little, pats my knee.

"This is what happens when an instructor comes in who doesn't know the full history on a client," she says. I experience three simultaneous sensations: (1) relief that she's not onto me; (2) discomfort over my rank duplicity; and (3) half-acknowledged despair that, once again, I'm wriggling out of the trap.

Toward the end of the program, "family night" is held. Mark and Sam attend, sitting in the same room where I've spent so many weeks, first accepting my alcoholism and then once again denying it.

"How does it make you feel when your mother drinks?" a counselor asks Sam. He's silent a moment, gazing out a window that looks over the courtyard.

"I like her the way she is," he finally says. "But when she drinks, she's not herself."

I don't want to hear this because I've already decided to resume drinking. I file it away under: Important Information to Remember. It's OK to keep drinking, just don't let Sam know that you are.

Chapter Fourteen

After the program ends, I meet with Michelle a few times to do some step work. I don't drink during this time, because *that would be dishonest.* She wants to mark my taking of Step Three—*Made a decision to turn our will and our lives over to God as we understand Him*—with a ritual. We decide to meet at the Grotto, a shaded stone garden at a local Catholic seminary that is a replica of the Lourdes Grotto in France. Inside a cave-like structure, hundreds of candles flicker before stone religious statuary. Michelle and I stand some distance away, at the back of rows of chairs.

"Why don't we get down on our knees?" she asks.

We're both in our work clothes—skirt, heels. We get down on our knees and join hands. The stone ground is hard; a pebble grinds into my kneecap. A few Grotto visitors glance over at us. It's a spring-like day, with warm sun filtering through towering oak trees that dot the property. I've already told Michelle I've picked Jesus as my Higher Power. Utter crap—but I know she's a Christian, and I figure it will please her.

"Let's repeat the Third Step prayer together," she says. Fortunately, I've memorized its archaic language: *God, I offer myself to Thee—to build with me and to do with me as*

Thou wilt. Relieve me of the bondage of self, that I may better do Thy will. Take away my difficulties, that victory over them may bear witness to those I would help of Thy Power, Thy Love, and Thy Way of life. May I do Thy Will Always. My voice intertwines with Michelle's, the duplicity of the moment a slick coating on my skin. Afterwards, we stand and embrace. There are tears in her eyes.

"I'm so proud of you," she says.

If there's a special place in hell for people who pretend to be in recovery but aren't, I'm surely destined for it. Does it cross my mind that I'm wasting this poor woman's time? Yes. Do I feel guilty about it? Yes. Do I realize that working the twelve steps of recovery while secretly planning to drink again is sure-fire evidence that I have a problem?

Hah.

During these few weeks, I attend the occasional meeting, if only to hear tales from the dead-enders to reassure myself I'm nothing like them. Like Satan in "Paradise Lost," the stories of drunken debauchery are far more interesting than the turning points of redemption that pepper so many testimonials. (*Yawn.*) Every now and then, an attendee, usually a woman, tells a story with details that dangerously mimic my own. When this happens, my breathing becomes shallow, my ears prick up: I'm not a drunk, so I don't like hearing evidence that suggests the contrary. One evening, a woman talks about how she worried she didn't belong in the fellowship, that she'd never lost a job or a boyfriend. Finally accepting she had a problem and getting sober was the best thing that ever happened to her. After the meeting, I approach her, half-dreading and half-hoping her story will correspond to mine.

"I've had the same experience," I say. Up close, the woman is a bit rough-looking: a chipped front tooth and fading black tattoos. Rode hard and put up wet, as the saying goes.

"Yeah, it's hard to get sober when you can fool yourself into thinking you're OK."

She holds a pack of Marlboro Reds in her hand. I'm keeping her from her cigarette.

"I'm always hearing these really bad stories, and they don't seem anything like mine."

"Yep. Listening for the differences. Been there, done that."

We're both nodding.

"I've never lost a job or had a DUI," I say.

"Yeah, me neither."

"Never had a blackout."

She pauses, looks down at me. Grins.

"Oh, I've had plenty of blackouts. Tons of them."

I thank her and breeze out the door. Check and double-check: *I still don't belong here.*

*　　　*　　　*

The day arrives when it's time to do my fifth step with Michelle: *Admitted to God, to ourselves, and to another human being the exact nature of our wrongs.* This is when you write down all your resentments and fears and share them with another alcoholic, to clear away "the wreckage of the past." The 12-Step program holds that resentment is the "number one offender" for drunks, the poison that leads us back to the bottle. Ever the dutiful (if faking) disciple, I make a list of all the people I resent, starting with my mother and father and then fleshing out the entire roster. Bad bosses, bad boyfriends, people who've been mean to me. As per the instructions, I jot down my part. The Big Book supplies examples. Was my self-esteem hurt? My pride? My sense of safety?

Fear is the other big bugaboo: alcoholics are said to be driven by *a hundred forms of it.* (Although to me, fear is simply a fundamental fact of being human, a universal problem not limited to drunks. Alcoholics just come to rely on booze to handle it.)

On a Saturday, Michelle and I meet for lunch and then decamp to her ranch house in the suburbs. I meet her husband, also a recovered alcoholic. He nods, then retreats to their backyard to clean the pool. Michelle and I sit down at a vanity in her master bedroom, our chairs mere inches apart. My damp hand clutches my resentment list. I'm worried this process might reveal me for the poser I am. The afternoon stretches out like a field of landmines, danger lurking at every step. We take the resentments one by one, excavating the psychodrama at the core of each. When we get to my father, Michelle slows down. I've underlined some thoughts in red pen.

"It says here you resent him for leaving you when you were six," she says. "And for beating your mother."

"Yes. There's also some other weird stuff around sex possibly. I really can't remember, just some vague images I have from childhood about my dad being weird with me about my body...and some *other* stuff."

I swallow hard. I wish I hadn't underlined that part. I get the panicked, suffocated feeling I always get when I think about sex and my childhood.

"But the big thing is he left without saying a word," I say, trying to redirect the conversation.

"He never called? Never wrote?"

"No. I saw him again briefly in my twenties. We got drunk together in a series of strip bars, where he was a regular. He used the dancers as models for his paintings. But one night he got mad at me for dancing with a Black man. He left me by myself in a seedy bar. So that was the end of that."

She considers this for a moment.

"And how did his leaving when you were a child make you feel? What part of you did it threaten?" She peers at me, concern hardening her pretty features.

"I guess it gave me the idea I'm not worthy of love," I say. It comes out as a croak. I've thought this before, in some inchoate form. But I've never said it out loud.

"And do you think that's true?"

Suddenly it's gotten a little hard to breathe. I wish she wasn't sitting so close.

"I don't know. Probably not. I'm not sure."

I'm relieved when we move on to my resentments against the patriarchy, which I can dissect with perfectly dispassionate anger. I talk about the Catholic priest to whom my mother appealed when Jack was beating her, who eyed her legs through a veil of cigarette smoke and told her to go back home and obey him. Oh, and those ridiculous rules about birth control. And no women priests. Abstract issues are so much easier to talk about than my personal history.

After an hour, we're done, my mask of fakery still in place. I leave Michelle's house weak with relief, my armpits soaked, marveling that even doing the steps under false pretenses seems to unearth some truths. That stuff about my father? I'd never gotten so close to the bone with any of my previous therapists. *Do I really think I'm unlovable? It's good I'm not taking any of this seriously*, I think, sliding into the baking front seat of my car, inhaling deep lungfuls of the hot vinyl smell. Michelle and I meet for coffee a few days later to debrief. At one point, she slides her hand over the table and grasps mine.

"I've done a lot of work with women alcoholics, and you're one of the most honest," she says.

"Thank you." That special place in hell just got hotter.

And then I just ghost her. I stop going to meetings. Michelle leaves one or two concerned messages on my voicemail, but that's it.

Attraction not promotion.

A week after my last meeting with Michelle, after almost six months of white-knuckled no drinking, I have my first taste of alcohol at, of all places, a church dinner party. I've already told Mark I plan to drink again since I'm not really an alcoholic. He seems fine with it. Or at least resigned. I think part of him has missed drinking with me.

The party is held at the faux-Tudor home of one of the wealthier couples from our church. The hostess has provided an array of nonalcoholic drinks; a pyramid of Diet Coke awaits me in the dining room. So does a crystal punch bowl full of purple sangria, slices of stained fruit floating on its surface. While Mark is engaged in conversation, I mosey over to the punch and ladle some into a plastic cup. For all Mark knows, it could be plain punch. I take a sip. The first hit of booze sends an electric charge to my brain. I set the glass on the granite counter in the kitchen, crowded with partygoers. I stand on the opposite side of the kitchen, keeping an eye on the cup. It could be anyone's cup. After less than a minute, I saunter over and take another sip, making sure Mark is still in the living room. Nothing bad has happened, no one is wrestling me to the ground, so I ladle a second serving. The satiny, hypnotic feeling comes on, traveling up my legs. By dinner time, I'm emboldened enough to pour straight red wine into my plastic glass. I set it brazenly by my dinner plate, waiting for Mark to catch my eye with a look. He doesn't. He doesn't say anything when we get into the car to go home. Nor does he say anything the following week when I bring home several bottles of wine from the grocery store.

Has Mark finally learned to *detach with love*, as they always drone on about at his meetings? Or has he simply given up? Either way, I couldn't care less.

I'm back, baby, I think. *I'm back.*

Chapter Fifteen

And things go well for how long? For weeks I am able to maintain control, or the illusion of control. Then comes the inevitable night when I drink too much and slur in front of Sam. Roll the tape once again: morning tears, agonized apology, heartfelt vow. (I always mean it when I say it.) Then back to meetings. Then the inevitable relapse. This happens half a dozen times, several when Sam is in high school, a couple when he's in college. Over time, I notice my once-affectionate son start to pull away from me. I tell myself it's just the natural disengagement of a growing boy from his mother, but deep down, I know the truth. *Didn't my stepfather's drinking repulse me as well?*

One of the worst nights: Mark and I attend happy hour with two of his new employees. He's now the executive director of a non-profit. It's two-for-one at a Mexican patio restaurant, a Friday night. The air is uncommonly festive. A soft breeze flutters around the tables, ruffling the paper napkins. The four of us drink several rounds, smoking cigarettes, laughing uproariously. It feels like the way Mark and I used to party before Sam came along. Afterward, at home, Mark and I decide to have dinner at an Italian restaurant. I sit on the bed and unsteadily pull on a pair of boots. I weave a bit walking to the car. At the restaurant, where a trio plays smooth jazz, Mark tells me to slow down with the Chardonnay.

"You're getting pretty drunk," he says.

"I'm fine, leave me alone." Tomato sauce dapples my blouse and smears on the tablecloth around my plate. By the time we pay the bill, the alcohol has reached peak concentration in my blood. I'm smashed—drunker than I've been in a while. As Mark drives, I leer out the car window like a brain-injury victim. In a doomed attempt to sober me up before we get home to our son, Mark drives around for an hour. He buys a chocolate shake at Wendy's and demands that I drink it.

"My God, you can't even talk!" He keeps looking over at me as he zooms down the highway, his face a mask of rage.

"You talk! You talk!" I babble like a deranged parrot.

When we get home, Sam is in his bedroom on the computer. With the impeccable logic possessed only by drunks, I shuffle in, deciding now is a good time for a little mother-son chat. I slouch against his bedroom door and mumble something lost forever to the sands of time, recorded only in the journal faithfully kept by the confetti God.

"Get out, Mom," he mutters. "You're drunk."

I awake parched the next morning. The first image to zoom in is the look on Sam's face as I weaved into his room the night before. It's an expression I'll never forget, a mixture of fear and disdain. I go into the kitchen, pour a cup of coffee, and swallow some Advil. Where is Mark? I'm sure to get an earful from him this morning.

Sam walks in. At fifteen, he's a vegetarian, a decision he made after watching a documentary on factory farming. He has an affinity for t-shirts with counter-cultural sayings. He's tall and handsome—my tragically brave son. Wordlessly, he gets a bowl out of the cupboard and pours in some cereal.

"I'm sorry about last night," I say, huddled over my coffee cup, a sick pleading in my voice.

"Whatever." He pours milk on his cereal, not looking at me.

"I drank too much at a restaurant, I admit it. I shouldn't have come into your room. It won't happen again."

"OK, Mom," Sam says, walking out with his bowl, retreating to his bedroom.

The next few days, I'm on tenterhooks, doing my best June Cleaver impersonation, baking cookies. I'm ruining my relationship with my son, some part of me knows this, but I can't stop.

How can I explain? What can I say that will make you, dear reader, not hate me? For an alcoholic or addict, the prospect of not drinking or using feels akin to standing before a 1,000-foot chasm and being told to jump, with every muscle in your body knowing that to jump is to die.

The day we brought Sam home from the hospital, I vowed to be his greatest protector. Yet here I was, causing my son the greatest singular harm of his young life. It's a testament to the powerful nature of addiction that it can neuter what may be the fiercest power on Earth: maternal love.

I want to temper these harsh words, hedge things to make myself look better. Even at my worst, Sam never had to scrape me off the floor. He never had to clean up my vomit. He had good food, clean clothes, and regular bedtimes. He graduated high school with honors, had a clutch of great friends, and got accepted into an elite East Coast college. I tell myself these things: he had a loving childhood and turned out fine.

But all I need to do is remember the look on his face that night in his bedroom, and I know better.

With Sam away at college, my need to control my drinking lessens.

Over the four years of his absence, my addiction progresses. We move to a smaller home in a high-poverty zip code to better afford Sam's college. Down the block from our house is a car wash and convenience store, permanently tagged with black swirls of graffiti. Police sirens make up the soundtrack of our neighborhood. Most of our neighbors are Hispanic and much friendlier than the ones in suburbia. Not far from our house is a large lake encircled by a walking path dotted with metal garbage cans.

At this stage in my drinking, I'm sometimes reduced to buying mini bottles of Inglenook wine at the grocery store and chugging one or two down when I know Mark is in Gestapo mode. I hide the empties in my closet, underneath a pile of shoes. I do the same with the tallboy beers I sometimes chug on the way home from work, on nights I fear I won't be able to drink enough. I can't put these empties in our trash bins, so on some mornings before work, I drive to the lake. Looking around to ensure I'm not being surveilled, I take the plastic grocery store bag containing several of my empties and stow it in one of the metal trashcans. Sometimes, a gaggle of geese will waddle up and watch me as I perform this furtive maneuver, their beady black eyes telegraphing an avian message: *We see you.*

Driving to work, a rational part of my brain flickers: this is not normal behavior. The wives I drink with on the weekends are likely not discarding their own clandestine bags of mini bottles in waste receptacles near their homes. But I push the thought away. I'm hiding the empties for Mark's benefit, finding empties would upset him. *I'm simply being considerate.*

Some nights, I'm reduced to chugging vermouth as I stand in our pantry. I silently scurry down the hall in stockinged feet, making sure his big, German head is turned toward the TV. Occasionally, Mark decides he wants to have a martini on a Saturday night.

"What happened to the vermouth?"

"Oh that," I say. "It was old. I had to throw it out."

I tell myself: If Mark would just relax, I wouldn't have to lie.

Sometimes Mark does relax. We take a weekend trip to Port Aransas and both get rip-roaring drunk. One night, I fall down a flight of concrete condominium stairs. I could have easily killed myself. Instead, we both laughed it off. I got away with a few scrapes and bruises.

We have dinner with friends at their house, another couple who are big drinkers. (Heavy drinkers tend to find each other.) All four of us get wasted. On the drive home, Mark pulls into a darkened strip center parking lot, where we have sex in the car. At home, we keep drinking. Mark is outside smoking while I pour us both shots of Jägermeister. For some reason, I'm squatting in the pantry as I pour the liquor. I fall over and hit my face hard on the ground.

The next morning, we're flying to San Diego for Mark's work conference. The first thing I remember when I wake up is that we had sex in a parking lot! And I notice the skin around my eye is very sore. Oh, yeah, I fell over in the pantry.

"Wow, what a night," I say to Mark as he prints out our plane tickets.

"Yeah, I feel like shit," he says. He doesn't seem mad at all.

"Sex in a parking lot!"

"I can't believe us." He takes the tickets and tucks them into the side pocket of his suitcase. *So far, so good.*

"It was fun!"

I touch the tender place around my eye. "I fell over."

Mark studies the red mark on my face. "You might get a bruise," he says.

"You think?" He turns away from me to fold a shirt, then turns back.

"How on earth did that happen?"

I shrug, trying to act like it's no big deal. "Not sure. I think I fell over in the pantry." He shakes his head.

As the day progresses, from taxi to airport to hotel, my eye grows redder. The next morning, I roll out of our hotel bed and walk into the bathroom. Mark is at a seminar. Standing naked before the mirror, under the harsh fluorescent glare, I can't believe what I see: a shiner to beat all shiners. The wound shouts from the mirror, its existence an accusation that can't be explained away. Women who drink normally don't get black eyes. Mark will be back any minute. There's no time to buy concealer. I put on my robe and sit on the bed, feeling sick to my stomach at the thought of what I know is about to happen.

He opens the door, laden with a USA Today and pastries for me. He puts the hotel key on the desk and walks over to give me a kiss. Halfway to the bed, he stops in his tracks, stunned.

"Oh my God," Mark says.

"That's it. You're done."

"OK, OK. I'm done."

That afternoon, we visit the San Diego Zoo. As we walk from cage to cage, admiring the toucans and snow leopards, the familiar rhythm beats in my head: *I can't stop drinking...I can't stop drinking...I can't stop drinking.* I look at our fellow zoo-goers and wonder if anyone else is dreading the prospect of never being able to drink alcohol again for the rest of their lives.

At noon, Mark and I sit at an outdoor café and order hamburgers. Before the zoo, we'd stopped at a CVS, where I bought Covergirl beige foundation. In the car, I'd flipped down the visor mirror and carefully dotted on the makeup, doing my best to obscure the bruise, which is now dark purple. Mark watched the whole procedure, grimacing. Now, the afternoon heat is causing the makeup to melt and absorb into my skin. The bruise is starting to show through here and there.

"People are going to think I'm a wife-beater," Mark says, pushing his half-eaten burger away.

"Well, I don't know what I can do about it," I say. I've barely touched my food.

"What you can do is stop getting shit-faced," he hisses, quickly looking to the side to see if nearby diners are eavesdropping on our conversation. Just an hour ago, he'd held my hand as we walked through the monkey exhibit. Now he's furious again. Up, down, up, down. We may be at the zoo, but I feel like I'm on a rollercoaster.

Later that day, we go to a baseball game. I want a beer badly, but I'm too afraid to suggest it. A young couple with two small children sits on the bleacher row below us. They're affectionate, holding hands on the seat back with their two kids between them. I watch them the entire game. They eat hot dogs and peanuts. They drink soda. They never drink any beer. *Who goes to a baseball game and doesn't drink beer? Maybe one of them is an alcoholic?*

There are no hits nor runs during the entire game, an apt metaphor for what's happening in my marriage.

That night at dinner in the hotel restaurant, I decide to risk it.

"Look, we're on vacation," I say, slapping down my menu. "Let's get a bottle of wine, and then that will be it for me. I'll stop for good once we're back in San Antonio."

I can see the gears cranking in Mark's head. He wants the wine, but he doesn't want to come off as a hypocrite. If I struggle with not drinking, he seems to struggle with letting go of our habit, enshrined over the decades, of fermented grape with dinner: the dignified waiter releasing the cork, Mark testing and nodding, the gurgling of the wine into our glasses. He shifts in his chair and glares at me.

"I think this is a bad idea," he says.

"I promise, this is it," I say. The bottle of red we order is overly dry. It's hard for me to enjoy because Mark tracks every movement of my hand with his eyes. Every swallow is silently commented upon.

A week later, I pick up Mark at work. It's Bible study night again; polite wine drinking is the norm. I haven't had a drop since San Diego. Nestled down by the emergency brake, wrapped in a brown paper sack, is a bottle of Cabernet. I'm waiting for Mark to say something. But he doesn't say a word.

On and on it goes. I drink, and nothing bad happens. I drink, and I get in trouble. When Mark and I fight about things that aren't related to my alcoholism, I tell myself, *At least we're not fighting about my drinking.*

Many days, I'm tired from drinking too much the night before. I find an excuse to leave work early, go home, lay on the couch, and watch Oprah. I know I'm endangering my career, but I'm on a conveyor belt with no off switch. I don't even care about writing anymore, about winning awards, being a good employee. My world has boiled down to a simple arithmetic: how much will I be able to drink tonight?

Mark and I grow more distant. He gets rid of the recliners, hoping it will stop me from passing out at nine o'clock. He buys a new couch. I start passing out on the couch instead.

One night, he sits down next to me before dusk falls. He picks up the remote and turns off the TV. *Oh God*, I think, *another one of our talks.*

"I feel like we're just roommates," he begins. "Like we just live together in this house with no real connection. It's like I don't even know you anymore." A sigh of relief: he's not talking about my drinking. Not for the first time, I tell myself the problem in our marriage is him, not me.

"What do you want to do?"

"I guess we could go see another therapist."

Within days we sit across from Susan, a grandmotherly woman in après ski boots and a cowl-neck sweater. I've become adept at presenting well to counselors: I keep my body language loose, telegraphing a posture of non-defensiveness.

Although, in reality, I'm more than a little on guard. Will Mark bring up my drinking? Of course he does!

"She passes out every night around nine o'clock," is one of the first things he says. *He lured me here into a trap.*

"And how does that make you feel?" Susan asks.

He ponders this a moment. "Abandoned. Like I'm in this marriage all by myself."

Susan spends most of our first session exploring Mark's issues with his emotionally distant mother. This is excellent: let's focus on Mark's problems. She asks him why he's so hyper-critical of me. This is really good! I'm starting to like this woman! She suggests that he stops going to his 12-Step meetings for a while, questioning the validity of detachment in our relationship.

"We don't want you to detach from Melissa. We want you to reengage."

Mark reluctantly agrees to suspend his attendance for the time being. Spectacularly bad advice.

I adore this woman. Then she turns to me.

"Tell me about your drinking."

I begin carefully, a climber negotiating a treacherous incline of rock. I've had some trouble in the past, I say, but I'm controlling it. It's not a big deal. I don't have any trouble at work. I've never had a DUI. Really, the only person concerned about my drinking is Mark. He glares at me from the other end of the couch: What a snow job.

"I have an idea," Susan says. "Go get yourself assessed for alcohol dependence and bring the results to me."

I have lots of practice with alcohol dependence tests and know exactly how to avoid the danger zones, so I jump on this assignment, going back to the treatment center where I did IOP.

The intake worker looks down at his paper checklist.

"If what you're saying is all true," he says (*ouch!*), "you probably don't have a problem with alcohol."

The next week, I proudly present the results to Susan, a pile of cow dung on a silver platter.

"Wow, that's really good," she says. "Most people would have put it off."

The alcohol issue now settled (for me and the therapist, at least), Susan gives us weekly assignments to do at home. It's all standard-issue marriage therapy stuff. We make a weak stab at it and then stop: neither of our hearts are in it. As the weeks go by, Susan becomes disillusioned.

"If you're not willing to do the work, you need to seek a different therapist," she says, her sweet grandmother act now over with. Mark sees her words as an opening.

"We can't do this work with you because we're just tiptoeing around the elephant in the room. Melissa has a serious drinking problem, and until we address that, no therapy in the world is going to work."

Susan and Mark turn their gaze in unison to me. I blink a few times. *The noose tightens.*

"OK. I'll stop drinking." I can't believe the words coming out of my mouth.

"Really?" Mark says.

"Really."

"She's made this promise before," Mark says, giving Susan a look that says, *Don't be snookered.*

"But I really mean it this time."

That night, while Mark is back at his 12-Step meeting, I swig the last of a bottle of red wine on the deck, miserable but determined. *It's time,* I tell myself. That weekend, we go to a steakhouse with my mother. On the way there, I tell her I've decided to stop drinking.

"Oh, I'm so relieved!" she gushes from the front seat. Unbeknownst to me, Mark has been telling her he plans to leave me if I don't get sober. I feel betrayed, but he sees in her a kindred spirit, someone who's been down this road before. My mother is a long-standing member of the 12-Step fellowship, staying in the program even though she and my stepfather divorced years ago. She likes to say she has a "black belt" in 12-Step. She's never commented directly to me about my drinking, but my two sisters and I have grown familiar with a common refrain through the years: "You girls need to be careful. Remember, your father was a drunk."

At the steakhouse, Mark orders a beer. He watches as my gaze follows a waitress's tray loaded with glasses of wine. *Get over it*, his look says. My mother orders iced tea. I tell her she can order wine if she likes.

"I don't need to drink to have a good time," she says, pious as a nun. I want to throttle her.

The next night, I walk into the bedroom. Mark is folding clothes. "What if I just drink on the weekends?"

He detonates.

"That's it! If you take another drink, I'm leaving!"

"Never mind! Never mind! I'll stop! That's just me being an alcoholic! That's what alcoholics do!"

I make an appointment to see a therapist who specializes in alcohol and drug dependency, part of my newfound goal to stay sober. Her name is Joan, and she comes highly recommended by a friend of Mark's in the program. Before our visit, I start mulling over this whole sobriety idea. I realize I have one last ace up my sleeve: I'm going to tell Joan that my problem likely stems from the Zyprexa I take each night for insomnia, on top of the one (or two) glasses of wine I drink. My only problem is that I fall asleep too early each night, upsetting my husband. I don't know if I can pull the wool over this woman's eyes. She is, after all, a specialist. I smoke a cigarette outside her office, leaning against the hot, ticking hood of my car, silently rehearsing my script.

Joan is preternaturally calm, her hair coiffed in soft blonde curls. Her office exudes nurturance: trailing ivy, an overstuffed couch, and a shelf full of addiction books. She sits down, crosses her legs, and regards me with a gaze that is both benign and inscrutable.

"Tell me what's been going on."

I lay out my pieces on the chess board between us. The Zyprexa, the falling asleep, Mark's sense of abandonment.

"I can see why he would feel abandoned," she says.

"Yes," I say. "Oh, and the Zyprexa has made me gain weight."

"Have you tried Trazadone? It's a good sleep drug for many people."

"Really? Maybe I should try that."

I tell Joan I drink around two glasses of wine a night, leaving out the secret imbibing, the little bottles of wine hidden in the closet, the slurring, and the impact my drinking has had on my son. I don't disclose getting rid of my empties at the park. I don't tell her about an incident that happened the previous summer, when Mark and I visited friends in Arizona. We drank the whole flight down, having free drink tickets, and continued drinking the rest of the evening at a restaurant with our hosts. The next day, I didn't remember that our hostess gave me a blouse as a gift the night before, after we got home from the restaurant. It's completely wiped clean from my memory bank.

"You don't remember getting that shirt?" Mark had said, turning around in the front seat on our way back from a day trip to Sedona.

"Of course, I remember," I lie.

My last blurry image of the night involved dancing drunkenly on the restaurant patio to a blues song.

I'm not sure why I didn't view this as my first official blackout. Maybe because it occurred at the tail end of an evening when everyone else was drunk. Maybe because I could hide it. Apparently, I didn't do anything stupid, didn't slur noticeably. But the fact is I was given a gift and didn't remember any part of it.

Denial is powerful indeed. Maybe it's the second-strongest force in the universe.

Joan hands me a fill-in-the-oval test that is supposed to determine if I have a substance abuse problem. I handily dispatch it, knowing which tar pits to avoid.

"Well, I don't really see a problem here," she says afterward, going over my results. She ticks down the form with the eraser end of a pencil, her face bland, revealing nothing. "There's some defensiveness, but that's understandable, given the situation."

I resist the urge to let out a sigh. *I'm off the hook!* I can feel myself unfurl in the chair. Relieved, my guard down, I start talking. For some reason, I mention the time Vanessa and I did cocaine during high school.

A slight frown passes over Joan's face.

"On the test, you didn't say anything about illegal drug use," Joan says.

Shit. I sit up straight in my chair again. Now I've gone and screwed the pooch. Will this cause my masquerade to come undone? Is this the loose thread that unravels the whole, moth-eaten sweater? I look down at my hands, trying to force a sheepish look on my face. Play it as a simple mistake. Nothing more than that.

"Oh. I forgot about the coke."

Joan looks up at me, her glasses glinting. She pauses for a beat or two. "The test specifically asked about illegal drug use."

Fuck. I look down at my hands, let my expression morph from sheepish to dumbfounded. I scrunch my brows together, as if I'm trying to puzzle out the tenets of quantum mechanics.

"It must have just slipped my mind. I only tried it that one time and didn't like it."

Joan takes her pencil and does a few calculations on the test paper. I hold my breath. Finally, she looks up.

"Well, that doesn't really change things much," she says. She relaxes back in her chair and sets the testing slip aside on an end table.

I realize I've been clenching my jaw this whole time. Joan delivers her verdict.

"I would tell you to just limit your drinking to the weekend, and then only two drinks a night. If you find you're not able to do that, it means there could be a problem. A red flag."

I nod briskly. "I'm sure it won't be a problem."

"And you might want to give the Trazadone a try."

"I'm going to call my doctor as soon as I leave here."

"And I want to see you again in a month or so, to see how you're doing."

I nod eagerly, even though I know I'm never going to see this woman again.

"Fantastic. I'll be sure to make an appointment."

I sail out her door. I can't believe it! A clean bill of health from an addiction specialist! Driving home, I concoct the storyline in my head: the Zyprexa I take each night "potentiates" any alcohol I drink, according to Joan. That's why I'm passing out at nine o'clock on two glasses of wine. It's as simple as that. Just a medication problem. When Mark gets home, I'm in the kitchen, frying bacon in a pan. I'm a violin, my strings stretched to the breaking point. What if he doesn't buy my story?

"So, I saw Joan today." Keep it casual.

Mark glances at the mail in his hand, tosses it aside.

"Really? What did she say?"

Keep your voice neutral and calm.

"She thinks maybe it's the Zyprexa I take. She said studies show Zyprexa potentiates alcohol and that's probably why I'm passing out at night."

"Really." Mark stands there, taking it all in, his face immobile. But he's not scoffing or getting angry.

"She wants me to try a new sleep drug, Trazadone, and to limit my drinking to the weekends," I say.

"Huh."

Mark goes into the bedroom to change out of his work clothes. Could it be this easy? Is he really swallowing this line of bunk? I feel a small spring of hope welling up. I actually dance a little jig as I stand at the stove. The bacon sizzles in the pan. When Mark comes back in the kitchen wearing sweatpants, he looks me dead in the eyes.

"So, you think you can do that? Just drink on the weekends?"

I take a fork, turn over a piece of bacon. This means I don't have to look directly at him when I respond. I may be a stone-cold liar now, but I do have my standards.

"Oh, yeah. It won't be a problem."

I get a prescription for the Trazadone, an old-school antidepressant. Turns out I need a pretty big dose to fall asleep. As a consequence, the medication gives me a constantly queasy stomach. My Zyprexa weight gain melts away. Since I take the Trazadone later in the evening, I also stop passing out at nine. This seems to appease Mark's concerns for a while.

As far as drinking only on the weekends: that lasts about two weeks. We go on vacation, which screws up the no-drinking-during-the-week plan, because you can't not drink on vacation, and when we return home, I find reasons to keep breaking that promise. The first time, it's a Thursday night. Bible study night, where everyone tipples. I'm getting ready in the kitchen, putting a bottle of wine in a sack.

"I thought you were only going to drink on the weekends," Mark says.

I crinkle the paper bag around the neck of the bottle.

"But it's Bible study night."

He softly shakes his head but doesn't say another word. That's because things are going well. My visit to Joan bolstered my resolve to hold it together. About six months go by without an "incident," even though I'm back to nightly drinking. I've bought into my own lie, that it was the *Zyprexa* all along. Unlike Mark, I know about the wine bottles in the closet, the Vermouth chugging, the empties secretly discarded at the park. Deep down, in some corner of my soul, I know that no drug in the world drives that kind of behavior. It's alcoholism, pure and simple.

Of course, the center cannot hold.

Chapter Sixteen

It's Fiesta, San Antonio's annual party held each April, a two-week celebration of culture and history—but mostly of eating and drinking. Mark's non-profit is operating a beer booth at the grand nighttime parade to raise funds, and I'm helping out. The Fiesta Flambeau parade is the big finish to this civic orgy. As the glittering floats glide past our booth, I quaff Miller Lite and pour drafts for the customers, taking their tickets. It's domestic beer, pure horse piss, but it's cold. Mark is busy running things. He's not drinking or paying attention to how much I am. Toward the end of the night, as parade attendees pack up their folding chairs and straggle to their cars, the grounds now littered with plastic cups and half-eaten turkey legs, Mark has to stay and break down the booth, so he approaches me with car keys in his hands.

"Can you give Marie a ride home?" Marie is a young deaf woman who attends his program. I nod and take the keys from him. I know better than to try and talk at this point. In the car, Marie struggles to explain how to get to her apartment as we speed down the highway.

"What exit?" I ask. She doesn't know. Maybe the next one, she says. It's hard to understand her because she talks the way deaf people do, and because I'm drunk. As we fly down the crowded interstate, I decide I want a cigarette. I use one hand to dig around in my purse. Searching for my lighter, I swerve out of my lane.

"Be caw-full!" Marie says, the panic stark on her face.

We exit near the Alamodome and get caught in heavy traffic. Inching forward, my foot slips off the brake, and my front bumper taps the car in front of me. The driver, a bearded young man, gets out of his car, walks to the rear, and bends down to see if I've caused any damage. Apparently, I haven't because he simply shoots me a look, then gets back in his car.

"Are you dwunk?" Marie asks.

We're back on the highway, hauling ass because I'm tired of driving and want to get home. I go faster and faster.

"Swow down! Swow down!" Marie yells, her hands gripping the dashboard. Finally, I deposit her outside her run-down apartment. She sticks her head inside the window as I start to ease away.

"You caw me when you get home?"

When I pull into our driveway, Mark is already home. We were lost for almost an hour. I work up a head of indignation, hoping it will mask my drunkenness.

"Fucking Marie! She doesn't even know where she lives!"

Mark gapes at me. His eyes shine with righteous anger. He stands ramrod straight, as if ready to fight or flee.

"Are you drunk?"

"No!"

I get in bed right away, hoping to forestall a conversation. The next evening, a Sunday, we sit on the deck drinking wine. Mark has that old look on his face, the one that says he knows I'm drinking too much. By now, I'm back to sneaking drinks here and there. There's been some occasional slurring.

"Yeah, Marie was mad last night," I say. "Mad that we got lost, and I was driving too fast." She may say something to him in the morning. I want to put my own prophylactic spin on the story.

"Were you drunk? You seemed drunk when you got home last night."

"I had a buzz, but I was fine."

"You know Marie likes to gossip. She's going to tell everyone at work tomorrow."

"Oh, she just overreacted."

Mark doesn't finish his second glass. We don't speak much for the rest of the evening.

Not long after, it's the night before we go on a ski vacation with a group of friends. I've had two drinks but want a third. *It's vacation!* Mark is still on the warpath from the Fiesta incident. Marie did indeed gossip about the night, telling everyone who would listen that I was ripped. So, while Mark's packing, I grab a bottle of beer from the fridge and go into the bathroom, planning to chug it. Suddenly, I hear Mark trundling down the hall toward the bathroom. Our bathroom door doesn't have a lock.

"I need to get my shaving stuff," he says.

"Don't come in! I'm on the toilet!"

It's too late. As his hand twists the doorknob, I leap from the toilet, jump the two or three feet toward the tub, and set the bottle on the drain.

The door opens just as I'm pulling the shower curtain tight.

"Why are you closing the shower curtain?" Mark asks.

"I'm going to take a shower."

He pulls back the curtain. There sits the beer, like a disobedient child in time-out.

"Unbelievable," he mutters.

Later, I crawl into bed next to him, penitent. "I put the bottle back. I didn't drink it."

"Whatever," Mark says, his back to me.

On the ski trip, Mark is fine with my drinking because everyone is getting toasted just about every night. On one of these nights, we're all at a bar after day-drinking at Lake Tahoe. I order a frozen drink that's supposed to have a shot of rum floating on the top, but mine doesn't have the little pool of booze. I start complaining loudly and try to get the waitress's attention. Our host, who is letting us stay for free in his gorgeous mountaintop home, tells me to pipe down. My drink is fine, he says.

"How would you know? You don't even drink," I say, sneering at him.

On the ride home, I start bitching about the host, who is riding in a separate car. I make fun of him and his teetotaling ways. I yammer on. Finally, the man driving the van snaps.

"That's *enough*," he says.

The next day, everyone laughs about my little public temper tantrum, but I'm mortified. On our last day, one of the men on the trip makes a crack over breakfast, something to the effect of my needing "individual counseling." I look at him, a forkful of pancake poised in the air. I don't say anything, but his wife feels the need to rush to my defense.

"You know how sensitive Melissa is," she says, chiding him.

"It was just a joke," he says. The exchange haunts me all the way back to San Antonio. *Are other people starting to notice?*

The tape speeds up at this point. A cliff's precipice is looming ahead, one I will fling myself from into a great unknown. Actually, I am pushed.

Sam comes home from college and stays with us for a few weeks before moving to Austin, where he hopes to find a creative job and adopt the ultra-cool hipster Austin lifestyle. Right after he unpacks his bags, I stand in the kitchen and explain why it's OK for me to drink again. He'd seen me sip a glass of wine at a Vassar pre-graduation party and had whispered his concern to his father.

"Mom, I'm going to love you no matter what," Sam says.

His words are comforting, but the blank look on his face says it all: *here we go again.*

I have only one mild slurring incident before he moves out. I come home at lunch the next day to see if Sam is mad at me. Preparing our sandwiches, I steal glances at him. He reacts as if nothing has happened. *Is he not mad because he couldn't tell I was drunk last night? Or is he not mad because he's grown accustomed to the idea of having a drunk mother?*

It's all about to become moot. Because just a few weeks later, I experience my first major blackout at the Majestic Theatre.

The cliff's edge is just up ahead. The jumping-off point is imminent.

When I finally push off from the rim, it feels like I'm dying.

What I don't know is that my real life is just about to begin.

PART THREE

WHAT WE ARE LIKE NOW

Chapter Seventeen

What transpires in the days following my blackout at *Jersey Boys* feels like a fairy tale—or maybe a modern-day parable. Things fall into place in some mysteriously interlocking way, as if preordained by a mildly interested deity, as if a soft wind is pushing at my back, whispering, "This way, this way."

Let me back up a bit. The day before the theater, a Thursday, I fill a prescription for Elavil. It's yet another drug, this time an old-school antidepressant, that I hope will end my never-ending quest to sleep at night. I'm tired of having a perpetually queasy stomach from the Trazadone. My doctor says Elavil might work. Once again, I'm prescribed a smallish, subclinical dose. I take it and fall asleep easily. The next night, after I get home from work, Mark and I sit in our recliners, watching the evening news, before heading downtown for dinner with friends and the show at the Majestic Theater.

"Do you want to stop in at the Gunter and have a martini first?" Mark asks.

The doctor didn't say anything to me about mixing Elavil and booze. The pill bottle warns against mixing with alcohol, but we know how over-cautious those FDA types are, right?

It's a warm night as we walk toward the bar. The sun has that golden, sideways slant it acquires toward the end of summer, ferrying the first hint of fall. We sit in the darkened bar and sip our vodka. When our glasses are empty, Mark floats the idea of splitting a second one (the drinks are huge), but I say no. I don't want to be drunk in front of our friend Mary again. We'd spent New Year's Eve together, and I'd gotten sloppy and slurry. *Not tonight*, I vow.

I drink several glasses of wine at dinner, barely touching my pasta.

Right before the lights go down at the Majestic, Mark brings both of us tall flutes of champagne. Then blackness. Then, lights on at intermission, and more wine. Then more blackness. I remember standing when the show was over, applauding a performance I have absolutely no memory of watching.

I emerge from my blackout to find Mark piloting the car down our pitch-black street. I try to talk, but the muscles of my tongue have been mysteriously clipped. "Shut up," he intones. "Just shut the fuck up."

In our bedroom, as he turns away and drifts off to sleep next to my sprawled form, his last murmured words are no different from the past parade of threats: "We're going to have to do something about this."

Morning arrives. As it has so many times before, the blur of the preceding night comes rushing back like an indictment. Only this time, there's a gaping hole in the tape, a Nixonian blankness. Mark stands by his side of the bed, pulling up his bathing suit. He's taking several carloads of clients from his non-profit to Canyon Lake for the day.

"Sorry about last night," I say. Silence. "It's going to be hot at the lake today."

Still nothing.

"I said it's going to be hot at the lake today."

"Yeah, it is."

He leaves the bedroom. I scramble into my robe and follow him into the dining room, desperate to smooth things over.

"Listen, I'm sorry about last night. I'm going to quit drinking. I'll go back to meetings. I really mean it this time." Mark shoots me a strange look, hooded and opaque.

"You do whatever you need to do." I follow him into the kitchen.

"I'm going to call Joan. I'll be honest with her this time. About everything."

Joan is the addiction counselor I'd seen six months earlier, the one I'd bald-faced lied to about the extent of my drinking. Mark fills a plastic bottle at the sink, the only sound being the rushing water. He turns off the tap, looks at me.

"We'll talk later, I have to go," he says.

He gathers his things and heads for the door. *We can't leave it like this*, I think. *I can't go the whole day not knowing where I stand. Is he really that mad? Was it really that bad?* Before passing through the front door, Mark gives me a brief kiss on the lips.

"I love you," he says.

OK, he loves me. There's hope. Maybe I won't have to quit drinking. Maybe the past will be prologue and within a day or week we'll be back on the deck drinking as before, safe and sound. There's a cold bottle of white wine in the fridge. Maybe we can drink it as soon as tonight? I'll make a lasagna. Yes, that's the ticket.

I walk across the street and buy a pack of cigarettes from the convenience store, knowing I'll have to chain smoke to get through the day. My hangover isn't even that bad. I read the paper, drink my coffee—but they're momentary distractions. My mind returns to the night before, a tongue irresistibly drawn to a mouth ulcer. *Why can't I remember any images from the show —the singing, the dancing? Not a trace. Did the people we were with notice how smashed I was? How could they not have? I couldn't even talk in the car.* I roam restlessly from room to room, feeling like my skin is two sizes too small.

By noon, I can stand it no longer. I call Mark.

"What do you need?" he says curtly, sounding professional.

"I just wanted you to know I really mean it this time."

"I can't talk about it now. We'll talk tonight." Click.

Tonight. He's coming home. He's not leaving me. We'll talk tonight. I vacuum the house, mop the kitchen, like a good little wife. I go to the store and buy ingredients for the lasagna, a wholesome dish made by a good wife who doesn't black out in theaters. The afternoon stretches into eternity. I smoke until my throat feels raw. Finally, the van pulls up in the driveway. I'm at the door when Mark walks in.

"Hi," I say. "I made a lasagna." The house smells like an Italian restaurant.

Mark tosses his backpack on the dining room table, which shines from the lemon oil I massaged into it earlier. I stand there like a third-grader, wide-eyed, ready to take my licks. *Go ahead, yell at me. I deserve it.*

"Well, here's the thing."

There's a look on his face that unnerves me: calm, unperturbed. Not a hint of the old anger. "Let's sit down."

We face each other on opposite couches. There's only a coffee table between us, but it may as well be the Mojave Desert.

"I've decided to spend some time apart from you, starting tonight. I'm staying with a friend."

Mark has threatened to separate from me before because of my drinking, but he's never gone so far as to actually arrange it. For a moment, I don't know what to say. I look down at my t-shirt and notice a big coffee stain on it. Or maybe it's wine. I touch the blotch with a trembling finger. Shouldn't I be dressed better for this occasion? My husband has turned into sand, and he's slipping through my fingers.

"But I told you, I really am going to quit!"

My voice breaks with the last word. It sounds lame even to my ears. Pathetic. Our two dogs start whining at the back door. They know Mark is home and they want to be let in so they can jump joyously on him, receive his pets and scratches. *Is my husband ever going to touch me again?*

Mark's face remains composed. Detached. He's scaring the shit out of me.

"I need some time apart, to figure out what to do. I think we both need it." He leans back on the couch, folds his arms across his chest.

Who is this person?

"How much time?"

"I don't know. Let's just... play it by ear."

I can't seem to move. My breath catches in my throat. Outside, the postman drops mail in our front door box with a sudden, metallic *thunk*. I want to beg and plead with Mark, get down on my knees. But apparently, I've made my bed, as they say.

"Okay. If that's what you want to do."

I'm too stunned to cry. The moment I've dreaded for years has arrived, although not in the way I imagined with Mark storming out the door in a blaze of fury. He is utterly calm. As we stare at one another, a separate thought forms at the back of my mind: *there's a whole bottle of wine in the refrigerator.*

He packs a small suitcase, kisses me again on his way out the door, and tells me he loves me. We're acting like strangers, polite and bland, patrons negotiating a bank transaction. As soon as Mark's taillights recede down the street, the full force of what's happening finally punches me in the gut: I'm being left. Abandoned. My safe harbor is no more.

Still, I don't cry. I can't cry. I walk into the kitchen and open the wine. I drink it on the deck, smoke the rest of the cigarettes, and stare dumbly into space as our two dogs romp about my feet, blissfully unaware that our household is imploding. I don't touch the lasagna, which emerges from the oven dry and inedible. After the wine is gone, I discover a tall boy, a Guinness (one of Mark's), nestled at the back of the refrigerator. I suck it down. I don't remember going to bed.

My first thought when I open my eyes in the morning is this: *history is repeating itself.* First it was my father. Now Mark. Only this time, it really was my fault. I drove him away.

Chapter Eighteen

The next morning, I wake dehydrated and shaky, an anvil weighing on my head. On my heart. The space next to me is cold and empty—an accusation. My husband is gone, too repulsed to share a mattress with me. I get out of bed, take some Advil, and make coffee. Again, I try to distract myself with the Sunday newspaper, but it's futile. A nightmare vision of my future keeps crowding in: I live alone in a low-rent apartment, dousing my loneliness each night with wine—the only comfort I have left. I've lost my job as a journalist. I'm back working in the men's underwear department at Sears. Because his father makes him, Sam visits me once a year at Christmas. He sits uncomfortably on the couch, eating the soggy stovetop stuffing and canned cranberry jelly I've prepared, biding his time until his obligation is complete.

Around midmorning, the phone rings. I dash through the house to answer it. It's Mark.

"Look, I may have sounded too harsh yesterday."

"Really?" A tidal wave of relief flows through my body.

"I don't want to divorce you. I want our marriage to work. But we both need time apart to figure out what's happening and where we're going from here. I'm reading this book that says a trial separation should last about six months. I'm thinking maybe we should start with a month."

A month. I can do a month. His words are a balm to my jangled nerves.

"I love you," I say before hanging up.

"I love you, too."

I decide to call Joan because the fate of my marriage seems to hang in the balance. I leave a message on her voice-mail, reminding her of who I am and asking for another appointment. "It's about my drinking," I stammer into the receiver. "I need to come clean." To my surprise, she calls back within an hour, even though it's a Sunday. We agree to meet the next day, on Monday afternoon.

The first gust of an invisible wind starts to blow, the first puzzle piece snaps into place. What therapist returns calls on a Sunday? What therapist can see you the very next day?

That night, even though nobody would be the wiser, I decide not to drink. I make a plate of bean-and-cheese na-chos and pour a tall glass of fizzy water. I take my Elavil and climb into bed with Pepper and Libby, canine substitutes for a missing husband. For the first time in almost two de-cades, I fall asleep without alcohol.

The next afternoon, I sit in Joan's waiting room, my foot wiggling nervously. I'm chastened, remembering the snow job I gave her six months before. I have no idea how she will react to my sudden reappearance in her office. Will she be-rate me for lying to her? Merely cluck her disapproval, then pass me off to a colleague, saying through judging eyes that she doesn't work with dissemblers? I'm about to leap from my chair and sprint toward the exit when her office door opens.

"I'd say, 'Good to see you,' but, since you're back, I guess the news isn't so good," Joan says, pulling me into a warm embrace. For a second, I rest my face on her shoulder, smell her perfume, a soft lilac scent. Then she stands back, her hands on my shoulders. She appraises me with a long look that is concerned but not hostile.

"Come into my office, dear."

The muscles in my neck uncramp slightly.

I lay it all out, talking so fast Joan can barely keep up on her legal pad. The secret gulps of wine in the kitchen. ("Yes, that sounds like alcoholic behavior," she observes). The times I vowed to quit and couldn't. My half-assed work with a sponsor. The blackout at the theater. The fact that my drinking bothered my son, too, not just my husband, as I'd told her in our previous visit. Staring at my feet, I confess that almost everything I told her in our previous visit was untrue. I read a handwritten letter Mark had given me that morning, detailing the ways my drinking had hurt our marriage, hurt him. When I'm done, I fold it up, and stick it in my purse for safekeeping. I smile at Joan. I'm a disgrace.

"Actually, he's left me."

"I see."

To my shock, the tears start to flow. Really flow. Joan hands me a Kleenex. Also to my surprise, I realize this unburdening feels really good.

"I feel lost," I whimper. Joan sets the legal pad aside.

"It seems to me you've broken through your denial," she says. "I think it's time you started praying."

As a counselor who encourages her clients to work the 12 steps, Joan isn't coy about bringing up spirituality in her practice.

She holds up two fingers and says I have two options. One is the easier and superior way; the second is the harder way. The easy way is to check myself into a thirty-day residential treatment program, where I would be immersed in information about addiction. The hard way involves outpatient treatment. I would go at night. Most of my classmates would be sent there by the courts. This second way, while less life-disrupting on its surface, is harder because you don't marinate for a full month in 12-Step messages.

"Yeah, I tried outpatient treatment once. I forgot to tell you about that. I relapsed as soon as it was over."

"I see."

I square my shoulders and lean toward her. She's drawing lines in the sand, so I draw mine.

"But there's no way I can do residential treatment. My boss, my work... they have no idea I have a problem, and I'm not about to tell them."

"I see."

"What would my co-workers say if I disappeared for thirty days? There's just no way. I'm a professional. What about my reputation?"

Joan stares at me. Her smile has faded. I want to be back in its sunshine.

"Anyway, if I were to go, and I'm not saying I will, when would I do it?"

"I recommend you go as soon as possible. Right away, preferably."

"No way," I say. "We're hosting a belated college graduation party for Sam at my mother's house Friday after next. I just can't miss it. If I were to go to treatment—a *big* 'if'—I couldn't possibly do it until October 1st." Joan rises from her chair and starts flipping through her Rolodex.

"All I can tell you is what I think is best for you," she says. She scribbles something on a post-it note, sits back down, and hands it to me.

"This woman would make an excellent sponsor for you. Her name is Margaret. You might want to call her tonight to see what she has to say about it."

Joan scribbles down the name and contact information for three different rehab centers in the Texas Hill Country. Below that, she's scrawled five things she wants me to start doing every day: go to a 12-Step meeting, talk to my sponsor, pray and meditate, read 12-Step literature, and read the Big Book. I glance up at her, trying to keep the acid out of my voice.

"I know 12-Step is a spiritual program, but I've always had a problem with the whole God thing."

Joan folds her hands in her lap, cool as a cucumber.

"Well, you're going to have to find a way around that."

We stand up and hug again. I make an appointment to see her the following Tuesday. I call Mark on his cell as I'm fastening the seat belt in my car.

"She says I need residential treatment." Silence.

"Really? Does she know how much you drink?"

His reaction is like lighter fluid on the residual embers of my denial: *Good question! Does Joan know how little I drink? Doesn't she realize I don't drink enough to qualify for rehab? Rehab is for the losers who drink a bottle of vodka a day!*

"She gave me the number of a woman she thinks might make a good sponsor. I'm going to call her as soon as we hang up."

I'm turning into the parking lot of Club 12. Margaret answers on the third ring; Joan had already given her a heads-up. The woman who will be my sponsor sounds effusive and warm on the phone, with an almost molten enthusiasm. "Yes," she trills, she would be happy to serve as my sponsor! A space, in fact, had just opened up on her dance card, and she plans to attend the women's meeting at Club 12 that very evening. "Would you like to get together in the fellowship room before the meeting? Thirty minutes prior, so we can begin to get to know one another?" she asks.

Another puzzle piece snaps into place.

"Sure," I say. "We can meet tonight. See you then." I hang up and pilot my car toward home, beginning to plan what I am going to say to Margaret. Chiefly, I have to convince her that rehab is a supremely bad idea, a massive overreaction to my little problem.

I sit at a long table inside Club 12's main fellowship room, watching the door, on the lookout for a woman who matches the given particulars: short, blond bob, casual pantsuit. People shuffle past, looking like travelers in an airport.

On this day, Monday, September 13, 2010, I am fifty-two. Margaret is closing in on sixty. In our initial conversation, she'll tell me she's a lawyer, though no longer practicing, the erstwhile head of a bi-national communications company. I spot her the minute she walks in. She leans over, peers into the smoking room. I make my approach.

"Are you Margaret?"

Straight off, I notice her eyes. They seem to shoot out beams of light, beams that illuminate the rest of her face, suffusing it with a kind of radiance. More than any words she will speak to me on this night, it's her luminescence that draws me closer.

"You must be Melissa."

We sit across from each other at the table. Margaret holds a worn-looking copy of the Big Book.

"Joan tells me you're considering rehab," she says.

For the second time in a day, it all comes out in a rush. I talk way too fast, but Margaret doesn't seem to mind. She just sits there, never interrupting. When I finally run out of steam, she offers a small, wry smile. "These stories never end happily, you know."

"Right now, only your marriage is threatened," she says. "Keep at it, and you'll eventually lose everything."

Margaret shares a bit of her story—the mess drinking made of her life, how she relapsed after a long period of abstinence, and the hard climb back to her current two years of sobriety. Then, she changes gears, waxing rhapsodically about the joy and happiness she's found through the 12 Steps. The light in her eyes switches to high beam.

"The promises do come true. I'm living proof of it, and there are millions of others," she says. "I'm finally comfortable in my own skin."

I can't imagine ever being comfortable in my own skin—without a nightly assist from alcohol. I can tell where the conversation is headed.

Straight into the danger zone.

"I like the idea of rehab, but it's just not possible." I give a my-hands-are-tied shrug. "My boss has no idea I have a drinking problem. I could lose my job."

Margaret pouts theatrically, holding up both her hands.

"Let's see. On one hand, you're dead with a job. On the other, you're alive with no job. Which one should you pick?"

"But my son," I say. "He'll want me to attend his college graduation party."

"Your son wants you to be sober," Margaret retorts. Then she whips out a special sponsor knife that cuts straight through my subterfuge. "Or you could *keep breaking* his little heart."

Somewhere inside, a tiny door opens. A shaft of light slips in.

"Are you sure this is going to work for me? That I can be happy without wine?"

Margaret's smile is splendid, blinding me without words.

"Okay," I say. "I'll give rehab a try."

We stand up and hug. As we part outside the club, Margaret leaves me with a mystical message.

"Know this: the universe wants you to be well."

"*Really?*"

When I get home, I call Mark and tell him about Margaret—her amazing energy, her agreement with Joan that I'm prime rehab material, given my history of trying and failing to give up the bottle.

"If this is what you want, let's do it," Mark says. He seems lukewarm on the idea, which puzzles me, given the grief my drinking has caused him. His enabler side, time-worn with practice, is beginning to kick into gear.

The next morning, I rise before dawn. My neighborhood is quiet and asleep, the other houses dark. I drive to my gastroenterologist's office for a scheduled endoscopy to see how much damage my acid reflux has wrought. Because the procedure requires sedation, my mother is picking me up. We're going to have breakfast afterward. As we sit at Jim's Coffee Shop, eating biscuits slathered in gravy, I drop the hammer.

"I'm thinking about going to rehab."

My mother sets down her fork. "You are?"

"As you know, I've struggled with my drinking for a while. Mark and I have decided it's time for me to get serious."

"If you think it's the right thing to do."

Do I? I'm still not sure. My mother looks down at her biscuit, as if it could oracularly transmit the sagacity of this plan. Perhaps she's worrying: What if word gets out that I have a daughter in rehab? Well-known as the co-founder of several women's organizations, she may be wondering how it'll look to the world if rumors fly that she's raised a drunk.

I'll discover later that many female alcoholics have fraught relationships with their mothers. It's almost a cliché. Remember how I said I resembled my father, the man she grew to hate? My mother had actually joked about it once or twice, that her feelings for him colored her feelings for me. We know jokes can sometimes hide ugly truths.

But today, my mother's compassionate side comes out, and we emotionally connect. It's a harbinger of the closeness between us that will take root and grow as the years pass. This will be especially true when she enters her nineties and develops mild dementia, when I take on the role of chief parent and shepherd her into assisted living and the waning days of her life.

As we walk to her car on this muggy morning after breakfast, she pauses in the parking lot, wraps me in a bear hug.

"I'm so proud of you," she says. Here come those tears again.

At home, I plop into my recliner, still loopy from the residual effects of the endoscopy medication. I have the whole day off from work. I take the paper on which Joan had written the contact information for rehab centers and start dialing. The first one is La Hacienda, the Cadillac of Texas Hill Country treatment programs. Dr. Phil sends his TV clients there. It costs around $30,000 for thirty days.

"When was your last drink?" the intake worker asks.

"Saturday," I say. It's now Tuesday.

"Where did you detox?"

I didn't need to detox, I explain. I never have withdrawal symptoms when I stop drinking.

"Well, that's going to be a problem," he says. "If you don't need to medically detox, insurance companies won't pay for treatment." I pause.

"Well, that blows."

"We could arrange a payment plan." But I know we can't afford thirty grand, even if it's strung out over months. The second rehab center says the same thing. Off in the distance, the drumbeat of denial begins to rumble.

"If I don't need to detox, does it mean I really don't need an inpatient program?" I ask the second intake worker.

"Oh, no," he says. "We don't agree with the insurance companies. But that's just the way it is."

Hanging up, I tell myself rehab wasn't meant to be. (The Universe, I guess, didn't want it.) I call Margaret, leave her a voice message that it's not working out. I call Joan, relay the bad news. She sighs on the phone.

"I guess your only option is the outpatient program. Again—I'm sorry."

I'm drifting off in my recliner when the phone rings. It's Margaret. I groggily relate what the two intake workers told me.

"Why don't you try Starlite?" she asks, referring to the third place on the list. It's where she did her own stint in rehab. I know it's an exercise in futility, but I call, just to show Margaret I'm serious about this whole sobriety thing. A man named Rick answers the phone. On autopilot, I explain that my therapist and sponsor both believe I need rehab but that I don't require detox, and I know insurance won't pay without it.

He asks a host of questions about my drinking habits. How long? How much? I give him the lowdown. When I get to the part about the empties in the park trash can, he chortles.

"Maybe you do belong here," he says.

"I'll call your insurance company, see if I can work something out," Rick says.

"Even without detox?" I ask.

"Let me see what I can do," he responds. I drift back to sleep. When I wake, the invisible wind starts blowing hard. I want cigarettes, but my car won't start. The battery is dead. So, I walk across busy St. Cloud Avenue and buy a pack at the convenience store. Rick calls back with a few more questions. While we're on the phone, a little girl who lives across the street rings the doorbell. She's selling Girl Scout cookies.

"No thank you," I say, waving her away, the phone at my ear. Then I call Mark, asking him to come jump my car. He shows up in a bad mood: it's a busy day at work. He spies the cigarettes on the counter and explodes.

"What the hell! You said you were quitting smoking! You've got fucking acid reflux!"

Trying to change the subject, I tell him about striking out at trying to get into rehab.

"Do you think you can just do outpatient?" He pulls off his work shirt, throws it on the floor. He's so tired of talking about all this.

"I tried that before, remember?"

"I don't see why you have to go away for a whole month. A lot of people get sober without doing that."

He makes a good point. But I'm not most people. I'm a chronic relapser.

"I know, but I'm worried."

"You really want to tell the newspaper you're an alcoholic?" *No. No, I don't.*

We go outside so he can jump my car. It's a blisteringly hot day; Mark's white t-shirt is soaked. I'm holding my cell phone in case Starlite calls back. Mark can't get the battery to ignite. He curses. My phone rings. It's Rick. I go into the house. Mark follows me. It turns out Rick has worked a deal where my insurance company will cover most of my $28,000 stint, but I have to come in tonight or tomorrow morning. If I go one more day beyond that, it will be too far from my last drink and the coverage goes out the window. I will have to go through "detox" once I get to Starlite, just as a formality. My heart starts to palpitate. *This could actually happen.*

As Rick is in the midst of explaining the arrangement to me, our doorbell rings. It's the little girl from across the street, her mother by her side. The woman tells Mark I was rude to her daughter earlier when she tried to sell me cookies. As Rick is talking into my one ear, Mark is barking into the other.

"Were you rude to her daughter?"

I shake my head, trying to hear Rick over the mother's loud protestations. Finally, the two leave after Mark hands over some dollars to buy cookies.

"It looks like I'll be able to go to rehab after all," I say quietly to my husband.

The ambivalent look on his face mirrors how I'm feeling inside: *Is this a good idea?* We're both standing at the edge of the cliff, looking down at the shoals below. What if there's no one there to catch me? What if my parachute fails to open?

"Do you want to do this?"

I open the box of Samoas and try to eat one, but it's like sandpaper in my mouth. I swallow with difficulty.

"I guess so. I've tried everything else."

He throws the jumper cables on the ground, sits down in a chair, and puts his face in his hands. He's got a reputation to protect. Mr. Non-Profit with a souse for a wife. Then he finally looks up.

"Then let's do it."

It won't be until much later that it hits me: if Joan hadn't seen me on Monday and if Margaret hadn't agreed to meet with me Monday night, I wouldn't have called Starlite until after the insurance coverage portal had closed. I wouldn't have gone to rehab, and the strange serendipities that happened—the strongest gust of wind that changed everything—wouldn't have occurred.

I call Rick back, tell him I'm coming in the morning, the butterflies in my stomach doing loop-de-loops. The second I hang up from Rick, my cell phone rings. It's my editor, calling to see if I am well enough to handle an assignment that evening.

I take a deep breath. The universe, evidently, has decided it's time for me to get real about my problem.

"David," I begin. "There's something I have to tell you."

Chapter Nineteen

The next morning, Mark turns our Honda SUV onto the long caliche road that leads to Starlite, a sprawling complex of aging buildings surrounded by rolling, scrub-covered hills and tall Texas oaks. I take long pulls from a bottle of water: the Elavil, though it lets me sleep, robs me of saliva. Last night, I filled a suitcase in a hurry, barely noticing what I was packing. Then, we drove to my office late, when my coworkers were gone, so I could craft an automatic email saying I'd be out for a month. I also sent an email to David, my editor, adding a bit more to our stilted conversation the night before: 'This is really embarrassing, but it's something I have to do.' On the way home from my office, Mark glanced at me sidelong from the driver's seat.

"You want to have one last party?" I'm pretty sure he was joking.

I shook my head.

The next morning, we pull into the Starlite parking lot.

"You're going to meet some real characters here," Mark says, pulling my suitcase from the trunk. It suddenly dawns on me: *I'm going to be here for twenty-eight days. Almost a month. With other people. People I'm going to have to talk to.* As we wheel my suitcase up to the intake building, the unreality of what's happening makes my knees go wobbly. *This is ridiculous: I can't be checking into a rehab.* But here's the nice lady behind the counter, handing me a breathalyzer. I blow. She hands me a plastic cup. I pee. She pricks my arm to make sure I don't have tuberculosis. Then, it's time for the official intake—mounds of paperwork, as if I were buying a home. Mark decides it's time for him to leave. We embrace.

"I'm going to miss you," he says.

"You'll visit me, right?"

"As much as I can."

And then he's gone. A sense of loss wallops me as he walks out the door. I'm marooned. Abandoned. Forsaken. Washed up on an island with God knows what kinds of craziness in store.

During intake, the worker asks me three times if I feel suicidal. Nope. That much I'm sure of. The nurse asks about withdrawal symptoms. Do I require medication to ease them? I'm tempted to say yes; a little Xanax (or whatever they give) might take the edge off. But I say no. A woman named Donna, a recovering alcoholic with parchment-paper wrinkles and red hair done in a fifties flip, walks me to a small room, where I change behind a screen into green scrubs. She affixes a blue plastic band around my wrist that signifies I'm in detox (or, in my case, "detox"). When I graduate from that part of the program, she tells me, the wristband changes to yellow, and I'll get to dress in street clothes. Donna shows me to my room, a utilitarian affair with two worn dressers and two single beds. On one of them sprawls an ample, mocha-colored young woman, snoring operatically. Her side of the room is festooned in tossed clothes, as if her luggage exploded. Donna and an assistant go through my suitcase.

"That's not necessary," I say. "I didn't bring in any contraband."

They ignore me, checking the pockets of my jeans, undoing my sock balls. As if I'm some hopeless drug addict who would smuggle a stash into rehab. Sliding her hand into one of the suitcase's pouches, Donna finds the Benadryl and Tylenol PM I've brought just in case the Elavil's not enough, or if the doctor rules that I'm not allowed to take it.

"That's just to help me sleep, in case this new medication I'm on doesn't work," I say.

Donna ignores me again, pitching the two bottles into a trash sack she has at her feet. I'm starting to feel like a criminal. Me, the big city reporter.

"Lunch is at twelve-fifteen," she says. "You can either go to the cafeteria, or we'll bring you a tray."

From the little I've seen thus far, the rehab is shabby and institutional. The Betty Ford Center it's *not*. But at least it's clean. After Donna departs, I wander into the bare-bones bathroom, where the shower drips and my roomie's cosmetics are strewn about the counter. I gaze into the mirror. I look exhausted, pale. Old. I'm in a bad dream I can't wake up from. As a social services reporter, I write about these places. I don't personally spend time in them. I sprawl on my bed and open up the Big Book someone has placed on my pillow. I read all the way to Chapter Four, "We Agnostics," which includes the line, "If, when you honestly want to, you find you cannot quit entirely, or if when drinking, you have little control over the amount you take, you are probably an alcoholic."

I've read this sentence before. It does seem to apply to me. I *have* tried to quit and been unsuccessful. But did I *honestly* want to quit all those times?

Is there an escape clause buried somewhere in that sentence? As I ponder this, Donna sticks her head in my room. "Lunch time."

I walk down a broad sidewalk toward the auditorium-size cafeteria, past a grassy expanse dotted with picnic tables. Two young women fall in next to me.

"Hey. What's your DOC?" one asks me, her face open and friendly, a silver stud piercing her tongue.

"My what?"

"DOC. It stands for drug of choice. Mine's crack." Apparently, it's a standard rehab ice breaker.

"Oh." I laugh. "Alcohol. Nothing glamorous."

They let me sit with them at lunch. Our conversation is strained, polite. I'm old. They belong to the young crowd, a lively group of kids who laugh, jest, and otherwise pretend they're at summer camp, not a treatment center for addiction. Most of the young patients, I'll learn, are at Starlite because of prescription pill addiction, especially opioids, as well as crack, meth, and heroin. I eventually find my place with the older crowd—a far less sexy group. We're just plain old alcoholics, wrinkled and shopworn.

When I return to my room, my roommate is awake, eating lunch out of a Styrofoam box on her bed. Her name is Loni. She's twenty-six, from Hawaii, and has three young children she hasn't seen in over a month. She's separated from her husband. Her DOC is cocaine.

"Before I got here, I tried to kill myself by snorting three eight balls of cocaine in a row," she says, as if she were chatting about the weather. "I must have drunk about thirty beers. I kept getting higher and higher. But I just wouldn't die."

I don't ask her why she wanted to die. It seems too personal, and we've just met. But there's a gentleness about Loni, a warm aura that puts me immediately at ease. Unlike with most women, I don't feel on edge with her. She has velvety brown skin and dark eyes, multiple tattoos, a lip ring, and a tongue stud. At six feet tall and weighing what must be well over two hundred pounds, she could easily pull off threatening. Instead, a vulnerability floats about her shoulders.

"Do you want to go smoke a cigarette?" she asks.

I have every intention of quitting smoking in rehab, what with my acid reflux. But I say yes, bum a Kool Menthol from her. By the next day, I'll learn smoking is the social glue of rehab. Almost everyone does it. Other than sitting in class, group therapy, or eating, it's about the only thing there is to do. Loni and I station ourselves at an outdoor picnic table in the detox wing, blowing out white plumes of smoke as an orange afternoon sun sinks below the distant hills, turning the day's end mauve and shadowy. Loni catches me looking at a line of white horizontal scars that march up the inside of her arm.

"I used to cut myself," she says, shrugging, again treating the dreadful as mundane. "It was a way to release my pain."

We sit together that night at dinner, as we will almost every night for the next month. I tell Loni my story: the sneaked drinks, being drunk in front of my son, the blackout. I'm starting to get my narrative down pat, and—*here we go*—I've begun to tell myself that the real cause of my blackout wasn't alcoholism; it was the residual effect of the previous night's dose of Elavil still lingering in my bloodstream.

Denial has trailed me to the Hill Country.

"But I'm still not sure if I'm really an alcoholic," I say, all breezy. "The way I look at it, I'm going to have to quit drinking no matter what, or else I'll lose my husband. So, it's a good thing I'm here. No matter what."

Loni nods in silence. If she thinks I'm full of dog poo, she doesn't say so.

That night, I drift off to sleep on the cushion of Elavil. It's not classified as a "drug of abuse," so the doctor has allowed it. Just as I'm slipping off, I hear a young woman kicking up a fuss in the hallway, as two staff members try to wrestle her into submission. She sounds like a trapped hyena.

"I want to go home!" she screams.

I know the feeling.

*　　　*　　　*

The next morning, Loni and I, determined to be sufficiently detoxed, shed our scrubs and fold into the general population. We request to bunk together, but for some reason, I'm granted my own room. Like the detox room, it is functional and utterly basic: bed, desk, bathroom, closet. The smell is old, moldy, with undernotes of the anxious sweat of God knows how many addicts. But as I unpack my suitcase, it feels luxurious, almost decadent: unlike the fifty-plus other patients, I have been given the gift of privacy.

The days at Starlite follow an unwavering routine. From nine to three, clients attend classes on addiction, the Big Book, and related subjects, all strictly hewing to the 12-Step party line. At night, we're required to attend meetings. In between this schedule and meals, everyone congregates at a large courtyard smoking area, complete with twin gazebos, benches, and a little desultory landscaping. After the night meetings, when the courtyard takes on the raucous feel of a college keg party, the smoke hangs so thick and white that people sitting in the gazebos become blurry outlines just a few feet away.

Mornings also include "group," small circles led by counselors who are themselves recovered alcoholics and/or addicts. The counselors also conduct one-on-one therapy with patients. That first morning, I meet my counselor, David, a recovering meth addict and alcoholic. Husky, with a scruffy beard and unnerving gaze, he comes across as almost catatonically laid-back. The first day in group, as seven of us sit in a circle in his office, David asks me to briefly tell my story. I'm a little amped-up and jagged, a daytime side effect of the Elavil that's supposed to lessen with time. My story comes out in rushed chunks.

"I'm sorry," I say. "I'm taking a new antidepressant that makes me sort of nervous." I take a drink of water out of my plastic cup. "And thirsty."

Seven people, seven strangers, stare back at me. Then an older woman pipes up.

"I can really relate to your story," she says.

"So can I," says another woman with a mane of beautiful hair.

"Me too," says a third woman.

Maybe I do belong here?

I decide to keep a journal during my stint in rehab. On the second night, holed up in my private sanctuary, I scrawl, "I really, REALLY want a glass of wine right now." What I really want is the entire bottle. Feeling restless, irritable, and discontented, I pad down the carpeted hallway to the vending machines for a bag of peanut M&Ms, a trip that would soon become a nightly ritual. That day, I called Mark on the pay phone during the allotted hour and asked him to drive up with cigarettes for me and for Loni, since she's broke. He balked at first—*goddammit, I'm in rehab, I'm going to smoke*—then agreed. The next day, I find a plastic grocery bag with the packs at the front desk. (Patients aren't allowed to see family except on Sundays and during Family Weekend.) Tucked into the bag is a pretty card from Mark. He loves me, he writes, and is so proud of what I'm doing. Also tucked in are several books on spirituality from the personal library he'd amassed since undergoing his spiritual experience in Houston. As the weeks go by, Mark would send me more and more of these books, praying each time, asking for divine guidance in which ones to send.

Against my better judgment, as the days in rehab blur together, I begin to read them.

Chapter Twenty

During my first week at Starlite, I have my initial individual counseling session with David. He slouches in front of his computer and types in my answers to questions. How much do you drink? How often? Etc. We talk about my problem with low self-esteem. He gives me a handout to read on addiction. It's all boilerplate counseling schtick, making me feel stuck in autopilot. My life has become like the movie *Groundhog Day*, only far less entertaining.

When our session nears its end, I flat out ask him the question that is bedeviling me.

"Do you think I have a problem?"

David pauses. "You do," he says slowly. "Like every alcoholic, you have a tendency to minimize your drinking."

I'm about to challenge him on this, but our time is up. David gives me a printout of his report on our meeting. Reading it as I walk down the hallway, I notice he included one of my offhand statements: '*I feel spiritually dead.*' I crumple it into my pocket.

In class that day, an instructor named Ann teaches about the First Step. "What are some signs of being an alcoholic?" she asks. I raise my hand.

"Most of the time when I drink, I can control it and nothing bad happens. But every now and then I get really drunk, and it upsets my son and husband. I say I'm going to quit forever, but I always go back to it. But like I said, most of the time I can control it..."

Before I'm done speaking, Ann writes '*loss of choice*' on the board. "OK, that's one of the signs. You try to quit but you can't. Does anyone know the other signs?"

Did she hear *anything* I said?

That night in bed, Big Book on my lap, my gut full of chicken casserole (the food at Starlite is unexpectedly divine), I read some of the personal testimonies in the back, categorized under the heading 'They Quit Before Things Got Bad.' These sagas sound a whole heck of a lot worse than mine. At the smoking area after dinner, I'd listened as other women spilled their own tales of excess. One quaffed handfuls of Xanax throughout the day. Another consumed five bottles of wine a night. Yet another habitually wrecked cars. *I don't belong here,* I say aloud, the words floating up into the cobwebbed ceiling. I start to devise a mental scaffolding: It was the Elavil that caused my blackout at the theater. It says it right there on the bottle: 'May enhance the effects of alcohol.' Over the next several days, the rationalization takes root and gains power. I decide to bring it up in group. When I'm finished, seven faces stare skeptically back at me.

"Have you ever gotten really drunk while not being on the Elavil?" David asks. His words carry a mocking tone. Well, *yeah,* I concede. Then he hands me a Big Book, asking me to read aloud the passage on how alcoholics will practice "all manner of self-deception" to continue to drink. *Whatever.* They just don't get it. That night, I call Mark on the pay phone. As we chat, I debate telling him about my new Elavil defense but decide against it.

"So, does being in rehab mean you're going to stop drinking?"

His question throws me for a loop. For a few seconds, the line is dead silent.

"I thought that's why I was here. I thought my stopping drinking was non-negotiable."

Pause. Mark's enabling tendencies travel like dark fingers over the miles separating us, burrowing into my ear.

"What you do is up to you." I think he's still trying to detach with love but hasn't quite figured it out yet.

"Tell me one thing: if I continue to drink, will you leave me?"

"I don't know." His voice veers into the irritation I know so well. "I really don't know. I'm just going to let you figure all this out while you're up there."

I want to gouge out his eyes with my fingernails. Mark doesn't realize that his wishy-washiness—or his detachment, or whatever it is—regarding my drinking contributes greatly to my own denial. That these loopholes he keeps giving me, or seems to keep giving me, prolong whatever misery it is we're both trapped in.

Two days later I receive a "get well" card from a friend in our Bible study group.

"Never in a million years would I have guessed you had a problem with alcohol," she scrawled inside. "But obviously you do!"

This woman is kindhearted. I know she only means to show support. But her card sends my denial into the stratosphere: *How can I have a problem when people I socialize with don't see it?* The resistance building in my mind forms into a snowball, careening down a mountain, picking up twigs, rocks, boulders. That night, I call Mark to tell him about the card. He uses the opportunity to tell me about the reaction of our friends when they learn I'm in rehab. Some clam up. Most are shocked. Some act as if I've been given a cancer diagnosis.

"You know what both Kirk and Rich said?" Mark says. "They said, 'We've seen you drink a lot more than Melissa.'" The snowball picks up a house.

"When I drove away from Starlite, I asked myself, 'Was I being too hard on her?'" Mark pauses. "I guess it was just my denial talking." I'm silent for a beat or two.

"Look," I say, my voice shimmering with anger. "The next time someone tells you they can't believe I'm an alcoholic, just keep it to yourself, OK? Because it's really not helping me in here. You're not helping me."

"I'm just telling you what people say."

"I don't give a shit. You're the one who drove me up here. Just keep these thoughts to yourself, alright?"

I trudge around Starlite, wanting to yank my hair out. I'm frustrated beyond words. Stuck in rehab with no business being here. At the same time, certain phrases have begun to burrow in. *Loss of choice. "I can really relate to your story."* Worse, the other women's personal backgrounds, spooled out over cigarettes in the smoking area, bear undeniable thematic resemblances to mine: early sexual activity, panic attacks, eating disorders, thwarted attempts to get sober through 12-Step, shame, and fear. Always the fear. Of being inadequate. Of not measuring up. Most of all, of not feeling worthy of love.

Histories of child abuse and neglect and pain surround me.

In these women's stories, I hear my own.

Chapter Twenty-One

It's a Friday night, the end of my second week at Starlite. With nothing better to do, I wander toward the Hope Room, where the staff plays movie DVDs on the large-screen TV. The Hope Room is about as cozy as it gets at Starlite: comfy couches, overstuffed chairs, and a large floor rug, where a gaggle of young people presently sprawl in various stages of repose. I sit down on the couch next to an older woman. She's got to be in her seventies. She smiles sweetly at me, then returns to her knitting. A staffer pops in *It's Complicated*, a silly romcom starring Meryl Streep and Alec Baldwin. I'm only half-watching, my mind returning repeatedly to my inescapable dilemma: *Do I belong here or not?*

A scene begins on screen. Meryl and Alec, separated spouses, decide to meet at a bar to drink and hash things out. As they begin to get toasted, the episode devolves into a montage: red wine poured into crystal goblets, the light glinting off the glasses. A cork pops off a bottle of champagne, the bubbles ejaculating into the air. Deep-brown brandy gurgles into two squat snifters, which Meryl and Alec drink from in deep draughts. I think, *I can't believe they're showing this movie in rehab!* The two characters stumble to the dance floor, where they fall into each other, just as Mark and I did on so many wonderful, wasted nights. It's too much.

I stagger up from the couch, craving a glass of wine so badly I feel physically sick. I burst out of the Hope Room and stomp back to my room, a pulse beating in my mind with every step: *Fuck this shit. Fuck this shit. This is just too fucking hard. I'm going to drink.* Then a second thought invades: But I can't drink. If I do, my husband will leave me. My son has already left me emotionally, or at least it feels that way. *I want to drink. I can't drink. I want. I can't. Want. Can't. Want. Can't.* At a level I've never known before, the hard truth reveals itself: I'm screwed.

In my room, I tear off my clothes, kneel down next to my bed, and bury my face in the mattress. Then I cry out to a God I don't believe in, because I don't know what else to do.

"Please, please, please. Help me God, if you exist," I whisper into what feels like nothingness. "Please take this fucking indecision from me, because it's driving me fucking nuts. Amen."

Then I climb into bed and go to sleep. Sometime in the wee hours, I have a dream.

In it, I walk up to the nurse's station at Starlite and ask, how long does Elavil stay in the body? Could it have been the reason for my blackout? The nurse just looks at me, with a face blank. I wake up and think: Wow. What an interesting dream. Especially on the heels of that prayer. Maybe I *should* go ask the nurse my question. Better yet, maybe I should ask the Starlite doctor, since doctors know more than nurses? But it's Saturday, so he's probably not in. I walk to the courtyard in the pre-dawn quiet for my first cup of coffee and cigarette. A gentle breeze rustles the trees around the gazebo, which I have all to myself. Katrina, an aide, walks by. She's one of my favorites, an elfin young woman who could be a character in an anime cartoon.

"Hey, good morning," I say.

"Good morning."

"Would it be possible for me to see the doctor on Monday?"

"He's here. He works on Saturdays." Another puzzle piece clicks into place. *The invisible wind starts to blow.*

"Really? I just need to ask him one question."

"Put your name on the list," she says, handing me her clipboard. I scribble it down and then head toward the doctor's office, propelled by urgency: *I need to know, and I need to know now.* When I get there, a half-dozen people already slump in chairs in the hallway, waiting their turn. I stand, tapping my foot. When the doctor's door opens, I lurch inside and close the door, protestations of "Hey!" and "What the fuck?" trailing me. The doctor and his nurse look up, surprised. The doctor is a wry, older gentleman with a grayish complexion. Recovered alcoholic, obviously.

"I just want to ask you one question," I say before I even sit down.

"Alright."

"If I took Elavil on a Thursday night and then drank the next night, could the Elavil from the night before have made me get really drunk and black out?"

He studies my face for a moment. "How many milligrams?" he asks.

"Thirty," I reply.

"Oh no, the sedative effects would have been gone by then," he says. He starts to say something else—"Now, there are certain long-acting *tranquilizers*..."—but I'm already out the door, flying down the hallway, searching for Loni.

Something profound is happening to me. As I run down the hall, I can't feel my feet touching the ground. A thrumming joy courses through my body. Colors look brighter. The air feels jazzed up and moves at high speed. I'm overcome with relief because at last I truly know: The blackout was completely on me, and blackout equals alcoholic.

And God exists. How else could I explain the dream?

I find Loni sitting in the back row of the Acceptance Room. I slide into the chair next to her and blow it all out in one exhilarated breath: The Elavil. The blackout. The dream. What the doctor said. She looks at me, her eyes luminous brown pools.

"Oh, man!" she says. "You've had a spiritual awakening! I want to have one too!"

In the days that follow, I float around Starlite in a kind of psychic ecstasy, flowing from meals to group counseling to meetings, riding atop a mystical pink cloud. Each day, I wake up inexplicably happy. Each conversation features a joyous new bounce. I don't go blabbing in group or at the smoking area about what's happened, because I know how squirrely it might sound. But every moment of my day is attended by this new sacred knowledge, which I incant like a precious stone: I am an alcoholic. *And God is real.*

The spiritual books Mark sends me continue to arrive weekly. During the day, I sit in the smoking area and drink the sugary red juice from the soda dispenser, shooting the breeze with the young addicts. At night, I hide away in my room, devouring the books Mark sends. Page after page, sentence after sentence, the words fly like flaming arrows straight into my heart, each one making sense where before there was only confusion. The same thing happens in class, where I begin to secretly worship my teacher Ann. Wine was my solution, but it's not anymore. Now I have a better solution: a Higher Power that, given time and certain actions on my part, will remove my obsession to drink. As they tell us to do in class, each morning and night I get on my knees and pray. In 12-Step, your Higher Power can be anything you want—God, Jesus, Buddha, music, nature, even the fellowship itself. It's a purposefully inclusive philosophy, meant to exclude no one. The only thing your Higher Power can't be is yourself—since you're the one who got you into this mess.

Floating along on my transcendent cloud of early sobriety, heady with natural endorphins, I decide that God, for me, is simply *light*. Light that is good and loving and true, a roomy concept free of doctrine or creed or all the other foolish ways human beings have tried to corral the ineffable since time immemorial.

Each morning, I spring from my bed. Acceptance is the answer to all my problems, as the Big Book says. Coincidences fall out of the sky. One day, I worry that prayer is already starting to feel like a chore. I bring it up at a speaker's meeting. The speaker says to keep at it: prayer will become easier. I go back to my room and pick up the book I'm reading. The next sentence from where I left off reads: *"There's no such thing as bad prayer."* The fellowship has a saying: coincidences are God's way of remaining anonymous; the trick is to be awake and aware enough to notice them.

Mark visits one Sunday, not long after my conversion experience. I've already given him the lowdown over the phone. He listens as I ramble on about my new faith.

"This is wild," he says. "Sort of hard to process."

The next weekend, Mark returns with Sam in tow. It's Family Weekend, when the campus is flooded with the people we alcoholics and addicts have hurt. Sam is still living in Austin, waiting tables at a restaurant. I've both dreaded and looked forward to this weekend. I'm eager for Sam to get educated on why his mother struggled to quit drinking, in hopes it might help him forgive me. Part of me—a big part—is ashamed my son even has to go near a place like Starlite.

On the appointed day, Sam stands in the intake building on Friday with his father, looking like bacon on a hot griddle. I give him a long hug.

"I know this is weird," I say.

"I'm fine, Mom. Don't worry about it."

I squire Sam around, introducing him to Loni and my other rehab mates. Given his truncated replies to their questions, I can tell my normally socially adroit son doesn't know how to act. I can't blame him. As we stand near the beverage dispenser, a young male addict approaches. Having chatted with him over cigarettes, I know bits of his story: recently kicked out of a prestigious private college in San Antonio over drug use, he's smart and pleasantly droll. As we stand at the dispenser, I mention that he and Sam share an interest in philosophy. For a few surreal moments, I listen as this young man and my son discuss the finer points of Kierkegaard, herds of patients trundling past.

I'm feeling jumpy about Saturday. That's when the notorious "communication exercise" takes place. Small groups of three or four families sit inside a classroom. With a counselor moderating, each family takes a turn sitting in a circle of chairs in the middle of the room, where everyone else can listen and watch. Each family member is asked to say two things they like and two things they dislike about the other family members, supporting the feeling with a specific anecdote and ending with how the experience made them feel. When it's our turn, the three of us face each other in the center of the room. I'm dreading the moment when Sam will go off on me about my drinking. Maybe he'll burst into tears or, worse, clam up and refuse to talk. Mark goes first. He dislikes my denial of my drinking problem (big surprise) and my emotional dependence on him (ditto).

When Sam's turn arrives, he says he dislikes how I've worried excessively about him from as far back as he can remember, and he dislikes it when I ask him if he wants an alcoholic drink at dinner. That second part seems to contain a deeper meaning, but he doesn't explain, and the counselor doesn't push him. As I'm walking my husband and son to their car when Family Weekend is over, Sam says something that fills my heart to bursting.

"Your drinking happened when I was already older, so I think it didn't damage me as much as it could have," he says.

We hug goodbye. Their car disappears down the driveway, kicking up a cloud of dust as it goes.

That night, as I drift off to sleep, it hits me: I can't re-member what my husband and son said they like about me.

*   *   *

I get my thirty-day chip in rehab. I breeze through Steps 1, 2, and 3, admitting I'm powerless over alcohol and ac-knowledging that only my Higher Power can restore me to "sanity." Step 3 asks adherents to turn their will and lives over to the care of this Mysterious Force on a day-to-day, even minute-by-minute basis, as best they can. Only Step 1 can be done perfectly. The rest are approximations. *We claim spiritual progress, not spiritual perfection.*

During one of my individual sessions with counselor David, I tell him about my dream and its startling aftermath.

"You've had a burning bush experience," he says, his eyes narrowing.

He's using terminology from the origin story of Bill Wilson, the program's co-founder. One night, while drying out in the hospital, the former stockbroker's room became suffused with a white light, which he interpreted as God. Balderdash or not, Bill never drank again.

But the Big Book states most alcoholics have far less dra-matic spiritual transformations. Called awakenings of "the educational variety," they unfold slowly, over time, but are no less valid for their lack of pyrotechnics.

Toward the end of rehab, I do a fifth step with another recovering alcoholic, an older woman who lives in nearby Kerrville, going over much of the same ground as I did with Michelle. A chain-smoking, latter-day hippie type, she tells me she can see into the future, among other psychic gifts. She's been sober a long time, and she seems perfectly nice, if a little nutty.

"I can see your aura," she tells me. "It's purple, the color of power. You're one of the special ones. You're going to help so many women." *Okaaayyyy...*

Then, during my last week of rehab, the pink cloud I've been riding begins to fade. Faint holes appear until the whole thing melts away, like cotton candy left out in the rain.

It starts with a bad case of allergies.

The gunk in my sinuses descends to my lungs. I start hacking up reams of mucus. As my health sinks, so do my spirits, and my faith in the miraculous. How do I know it was God speaking to me in that dream? What if it was just my subconscious, the detritus of my mind talking to itself as I slept?

That very afternoon, I pick up the book I'm reading, *Celebration of Discipline* by Richard Foster, a Quaker theologian, and read this sentence: 'For fifteen centuries, Christians overwhelmingly considered dreams as a natural way in which the spiritual world broke into our lives.' The book goes on to say the practice of viewing dreams as a way to discern God's will fell out of favor with the advent of rationalism and psychology. I read the paragraph over and over. What are the odds? The very day I'm besieged by doubts that God spoke to me in a dream, I come upon a sentence in a book I just happen to be reading that says for hundreds of years, people believed God spoke to them through dreams?

I look up at the ceiling.

"Alright," I say. "I get it."

The next day in group, I talk about the dream, keeping things vague, fearing everyone will think I'm nuts. I talk about my doubt and finding the passage in the Foster book about God and dreams.

Carter, a young man who had only recently arrived at Starlite, reeking of alcohol as he stood next to me for the Serenity Prayer, turns to me with a look of utter sincerity.

"Man, somebody is trying to talk to you," he says.

*   *   *

My last day in rehab arrives. I pack my belongings and bid a silent goodbye to the room where my big Turning Point happened. Already, the disquiet is settling in: Will what went down in my dorm room remain clear in my mind after I pass through the gates of Starlite? More importantly, will my nightly desire to drink, knocked into remission since the dream, return with a vengeance once I'm in the real world? With its workaday stresses and strain? Its glistening bottles of Chardonnay? Will my fledgling spirituality dissipate like Hill Country mist once exposed to the rigors of reality?

I smoke one last cigarette in the gazebo, empty because everyone is in class. Shaded from the September sun, the gazebo silent for once, remnants of conversations I've had over the past month swirl around me, making my throat tight. Images of the people I've met at Starlite parade before me. The blue-eyed young woman with the little-girl voice: her father introduced her to heroin. Another girl in her late teens, chatty and effervescent, who breezed around campus as if it were sorority rush: it was her fifth stint in treatment. The young Black woman who finally confessed that her substance of choice was crack, ashamed of its ghetto reverberations. What will become of them? Will they stay sober? Alas, the statistics aren't on their side. So many stories. So much pain.

Am I the only person in history who doesn't want to leave rehab?

I walk to intake with my suitcase, feeling like it was a million years ago when Mark dropped me off. The room remains as it was the first time I saw it: the same blocky wood furniture, wall hangings, fake palm in the corner. How could things have stayed the same when I've changed so much?

Mark is already standing at the check-in counter, smiling.

"You ready to go?" he says.

174

I kiss him, roll my luggage his way.

"I suppose. I have to say goodbye to Loni first."

I find her sitting in the back row of the Acceptance Room, working on a collage. I ask Ann if she can step outside for just a minute, to say goodbye. In the hallway, I hand her a carton of Marlboro Reds, my parting gift. I put my hand on her cheek.

"I'm never going to forget you," I say.

"I won't forget you either." She tucks the carton under her arm.

"Stay sober, my friend."

"I'm going to try. You, too."

"Let's stay in touch," I say, already knowing we won't.

Mark loads my suitcase into the back of our car, and just like that, we're off. Butterflies ping-pong around my stomach as we drive down the long road. I turn and look out the back window, watching the beige buildings recede.

"I'm done," Mark says. We've just pulled onto the highway.

"What do you mean?"

"I'm done drinking."

We hadn't had this conversation the entire time I was in rehab. I wasn't sure how this new arrangement was going to work. Alcohol had been the leitmotif of our marriage from the start. How was the symphony going to sound now with only one instrument playing?

I gaze at Mark's profile, his noble Roman nose. His hands grip the steering wheel.

"Really?"

"Yeah, I don't need it. It's not good for me. I want to support you."

I reach over, squeeze his arm. My old safe harbor is back, and I swim gratefully into port.

"Thank you. That would really help me."

"We're in this together, Ba," he says, taking up my hand and giving it a kiss.

175

As our car sailed toward San Antonio, we figured all our problems were behind us now that I'd stopped drinking.

Ha.

Chapter Twenty-Two

My first weekend back, I have a session with Margaret, the woman who suggested I go to rehab. The woman who would become my sponsor. We sit in Club 12's dingy smoking room, a glassed-in area that feels like a carcinogen-rich terrarium. I sit across from her and disgorge all the things that happened in rehab. My words come out in an excited rush. "That's amazing," she says, not quite as bowled over as I'd hoped.

Perhaps miracles (if that's indeed what happened to me) are only powerful to the person who's experienced them.

Margaret has asked me to write down examples of my powerlessness and unmanageability. We sit at our table, the stained piece of notebook paper between us, and go over the familiar litany. The secret drinking. The hidden bottles. The slurring. The angry husband. The hurt child. *Blah-blah-blah.*

"I wanted you to get this on paper, so you will have it if you start to waver," Margaret says.

"Oh, I'm not going to waver." She smiles that sun-lit smile.

"All the same, keep it close by."

"You don't have to worry about me."

"Whatever you do, don't put any alcohol in your body."

"Not even a chance."

"And I want you to do ninety meetings in ninety days."

"I am on it. I so want this."

"I want you to call me every day to check in. Even when the phone weighs fifty pounds."

"I'll do whatever you say."

I'm willing to follow instructions, having been beaten into a state of submission by the tyrant alcohol. It's what Margaret calls "the gift of desperation." A gift I'd never imagined being happy to receive.

Despite all my newcomer hubris, however, denial isn't quite through with me.

For in the days to come, waver I would.

*   *   *

My first day back at work arrives. For weeks, I'd been dreading this moment. I wake up before dawn that Monday morning. The second my eyes open, the reptilian part of my brain spurts adrenaline into my bloodstream, sending little zings of alarm up my legs. I picture myself doing the walk of shame down the center aisle of the newsroom, under the withering gaze of my colleagues. Above their heads, giant thought bubbles form: *There she is, the drunk. We always knew there was something wrong with her.* Surely word has gotten out that I went to rehab. No doubt my co-workers have held multiple water cooler pow-wows, dissecting my manifold personality defects.

The second fear is greater: What happens after work when the wine bottle beckons? I'm afraid to move. Maybe if I don't move, I can stay in bed forever.

"You awake?" says Mark.

"Looks like it."

He climbs out of bed, stretches, and goes into the kitchen to make a pot of coffee. When its aroma hits the air, I reluctantly pull on my robe. We take our steaming mugs outside to the deck, where darkness still enveloped the back-yard. The dogs dance around in circles, unaccustomed to our early-morning presence in their domain. We light cigarettes.

"How're you feeling?" Mark asks.

"When I first woke up, I was scared about going back to work. But now I'm a little excited. My new life is starting; is that weird?"

"No, it sounds pretty good."

"I have nothing to be ashamed of, right?"

"Absolutely not." He taps his cigarette against the ash-tray.

"I was sick, so I got help." I'm practicing on him.

"That's exactly right."

"So, if people are going to judge me, they can just go fuck themselves, right?"

"Definitely." Mark leans back, stretches his arms above his head. I know from experience he has limits with this sort of navel-gazing.

"And people *are* going to judge me, right? For going to rehab?"

"Don't worry about them."

"That's easy for you to say."

Mark stubs his cigarette, swallows the last of his coffee.

"I have an idea. Let's pray."

He stretches his hands across the glass tabletop toward me. Even with my epiphany in rehab, the whole praying thing still feels artificial to me—like I'm a kid playing dress-up. But I've been beaten into a state of submission, willing to do the uncomfortable. I slide my hands into his. We bow our heads.

"Please make today easy for Melissa. Take away her fear, God, and make her strong."

"I have nothing to be ashamed of," I say, a tremor in my voice. "Give me the strength to be honest about where I've been when people ask. Amen."

As the first tinges of pink appear in the sky, Mark reads aloud from the *Daily Reflections* and *Twenty-Four Hours*, a 12-Step book of meditations. As he reads, I repeat to myself: *Nothing to be ashamed of, nothing to be ashamed of, nothing to be ashamed of.*

I get to work early, before anyone else has arrived. In the dusky newsroom, I slog through a month of emails. None, I note with relief, are from any sources wondering where in the hell I disappeared to. An hour ticks by. People start to trickle in, including my editor David, an unflappable man. He unlocks the door to his office and goes inside. I take a few deep breaths, silently repeat the Serenity Prayer, and go stand in his doorway.

"Hi," I say with a quivering smile. "I'm back."

"Welcome back," he says. "Have a seat."

My editor tells me he didn't disclose to any staff where I was, short of the top brass. I feel I owe him some sort of explanation, given the rushed nature of my exit. I deliver a condensed version of my alcoholism story. I was never drunk at work, I tell him, and that's the God's honest truth. I just had to stop drinking, and I couldn't. Oh, I had this really big blackout at the Majestic Theater. That was sort of my bottom. I smile again. My editor listens respectfully, not asking any questions. I can tell this little talk is making him uncomfortable. I wrap it up, folding my hands in my lap.

"Well, welcome back," he says. "Everything is fine. No one in upper management said anything about your absence, so let's just get back to work."

"OK. I'm ready."

I blow out of his office, my chest filling with air. *Could it really be this easy?*

I sit back down at my cubicle. By now, two of my male co-workers who sit in the adjoining cubicle have arrived. I'm still fairly new to the "pod" and don't know either of them well. One is friendly, a mild-mannered religion writer.

The other is a somewhat taciturn investigative reporter who sits right across from my desk. Though we face each other—literally, our faces are mere feet away—we rarely speak, not even a hello in the morning. Because of this, I've decided he despises me. This makes me second-guess anything I say to him, in the rare instances when we speak. So, of course, everything I say comes out weird. I sit down at my desk. They both look at me.

"Where've you been?" the religion writer asks.

"I've been at rehab," I say. Pause. "For alcoholism."

The investigative reporter pulls an incredulous mug: "What?"

"That's right," I say, squaring my shoulders. "I'm not going to lie about it."

The religion writer smiles and nods his head. "For sure. No need to lie." And that's it. They go back to work.

Really? *That's it?* They don't want to hear the gory details, which I find so endlessly gripping? The only other coworker who asks where I've been is the gardening editor. When I tell her, her face breaks into a beatific smile: "Congratulations," she gushes. Not a single other soul asks about my absence. It seems I can be gone for a month and cause nary a ripple in the newsroom ecosystem. Not even the chief newsroom gossip, a woman who trades in the foibles of others as if they were prized truffles, has spread any rumors about me. I find the whole situation vaguely insulting.

You mean I'm not *the center of the universe?*

*　　　*　　　*

It's week two of my post-rehab sobriety. I sit across the table from two old work friends, Michelle and Rich, as we await our entrées inside a trendy lunch spot. Hanging green plants, smooth jazz soundtrack. Unlike most of my colleagues, they're deeply interested in my sojourn to rehab. (They love me, but they're also nosy reporters.) Their eyes grow wide over bowls of tomato basil soup as I recount the tawdry details of my drinking life, since there's no place to hide anymore.

My eyes cut repeatedly to my cell phone next to my plate. I've left a voicemail with that doctor from my church who put me on Zyprexa years before, saying I had an urgent question. The question is this: Could the Elavil have caused my blackout?

As incredible as it may seem, I'm back to doubting whether I'm truly an alcoholic. If anyone questions the baffling nature of addiction, the persistence of my delusion should offer convincing proof. As I sit recounting to my friends the many ways in which I'm an alcoholic, my eyes continue to dart sideways, praying for a phone call that will argue otherwise.

It started innocently enough.

A day after my return to work, in between phone interviews, I sit at my desk, a teensy thought forming in my brain: Now that I'm in the wider world, what harm could there be in researching the interaction of Elavil and alcohol? I am, after all, a reporter: research is what I do. I call up Google, type in "Elavil and alcohol." And, by golly, up pops a website on drug interactions, stating that, yes indeed, Elavil can enhance the effects of alcohol. That's all it says. But wait, here's another website that lets you put your question before an actual live doctor, for just $38. I type in my credit card number and tap out my query: Can taking 30 milligrams of Elavil the night before having six drinks cause a blackout? For the next ten minutes, I check my email inbox obsessively. Finally, the reply pops up: Yes, the drug could play a role.

That's it. No explanation. But it's enough to throw me full force back into the purgatory I inhabited before rehab: *Can I drink? Were those thirty days in treatment simply the result of a tragic misunderstanding?*

I debate sending the doctor's response to Mark. After a few moments, I hit send because he needs to see this, but I need more confirmation. I require a real doctor to bolster my case. Feeling slightly icky, I leave another message with the doctor from my church, posing the question and trying to keep my voice casual. The rest of the afternoon passes in a state of torture as I await his return call. As I hustle out of the office for an evening assignment, my cell phone finally rings.

"Well, Elavil stays longer in the body than some other drugs," the doctor says warily. "It could be a complicating factor, but it sounds to me like alcohol is the main driving player here. I suggest you get some help." There's a coldness in his voice I haven't heard before.

I don't tell him I've already gotten the help. "I appreciate that."

However, I'm still not placated. What does the doctor know?

That night, I'm wiping down the kitchen counter when Mark comes home from work. He puts his briefcase down and stands across from me, skipping our customary kiss hello.

"What was that email about from the online doctor?"

I turn on the hot water, rinse the sponge, and affect an air of casual indifference. "Oh, nothing. I'm just checking some stuff."

"What do you mean, 'Checking some stuff?'"

"I was curious if the Elavil had some role to play in how I blacked out at the Majestic."

"Why? What difference would it make?" He leans his hip against the counter, an oh-God-not-this-again look in his eyes.

"It doesn't make any difference. I was just curious." I'm traversing a tightrope, my feet slipping with each step.

"If it doesn't make any difference, why are you curious?"

"I don't know, Mark," I say, throwing the sponge in the sink. "Just forget that I did it, okay? Forget it. It's not a big deal."

He's not going to let this drop. Mark the Enabler has been replaced by Mark the Hard Ass.

"It reminded me of how you used to be—before rehab. Always trying to find some excuse to keep drinking."

"Don't worry about it. I'm fine."

We don't talk about it the rest of the evening, which I spend drenched in a familiar feeling: the sense that I'm hiding something from Mark. It feels wretched. I'm so glad Sam isn't around to witness this.

The next night, I have my weekly meeting with Margaret at Club 12. We're supposed to work on Step Two. I know she's not going to like it, but I feel a need to come clean. I tell her about my Google search, etc. As the words leave my mouth, her sunny smile fades, replaced by what I will come to call her bullshit-detector look: unflinching gaze, set jaw. On the table before us sits the crinkly paper where I've listed the many examples of how booze wrecked my life.

Margaret waits a hair's breadth before responding.

"People don't pack their bags and go to rehab because of one blackout," she says, smiling snidely as if I'm three cards short of a full deck. (Are sponsors allowed to be sarcastic?) Then, she bends over the notebook page. Her hands make a lawyerly flourish, as if she were back in the courtroom, delivering a damaging summation.

"Speaking as a lawyer, this is what we would call a preponderance of the evidence. You're not a social drinker. The blackout was just a tiny piece of your experience. What would you have done if the doctor had said the Elavil was the only cause?" I stare dully at her.

"I would have been unhappy. I want to stay on the path of the Sunlight of the Spirit." (*Do I believe this? I think I do.*)

Like a reaper with a scythe, Margaret uses her courtroom skills to shred my denial. When our hour is done, she stands up and hugs me heartily. Even though she had to set me straight, there's no judgment in her demeanor. I'd learn over time that there was nothing I could do that would push Margaret away from me.

Driving home, I roll our session over in my mind. Some facts couldn't be disputed. Maybe God (*or whatever*) put the Elavil in my life to accelerate my descent to the bottom. To speed up the whole sordid affair.

A couple of days later, Mark and I meet with Dr. B, an after-care counselor from Starlite we've decided to see for marriage counseling. We've heard the statistics showing many married couples in which the alcoholic gets sober eventually divorce, unless the nonalcoholic gets into recovery, too. Mark is back going to his own 12-Step meetings, in hopes that we can avoid this fate. Dr. B is an even-keeled, open-faced guy with a full-bellied laugh. Crew-cut and ripped, with tons of sobriety, he looks like a sexy Marine. I like him a lot. Mark and I sink down into his leather couch and talk about how my drinking affected our marriage. Then, as I feared he might, Mark brings up my Elavil research.

"You came out of rehab fresh and strong and convicted in your disease," Dr. B. says. "Why did you feel the need to research Elavil? What triggered that? What was behind it?"

His face is placid. I sit there for a few seconds, feeling itchy. "I don't know. I really don't know. Maybe a desire to drink?"

"No," Dr. B says.

"Maybe fear?" I'm learning fear is always a good answer to any recovery-related question.

"No." It's quiet in his office. His wall clock ticks. I begin to feel mildly retarded.

"Think back to what you were thinking when you typed 'Elavil' into your search engine," he says.

A few seconds pass. It dawns on me: The same thought process that tripped me up each time I relapsed in the past prompted my frantic search for a loophole. It's all rooted in memories of all the times I drank and nothing bad happened. I say this out loud. Dr. B sits back in his chair, his eyes never leaving my face.

"What do you think about this line of thought now?" he asks.

I throw up my hands, defeated. "It's a lie."

"You've got to smash all that," Dr. B says coolly, one drunk to another, which is how the program works. "Smash it to smithereens."

I smash it. *Smash that shit to a billion little pieces.* When we leave Dr. B's office, I experience the floating sensation I did in rehab. The therapy session would prove the last time I'd question my status as a problem drinker.

*   *   *

But not necessarily the last time I noticed others drinking. After our session with Dr. B, Mark and I go to our favorite neighborhood Italian spot. Like a special ops agent, I scan the tables around me. Three o'clock: a couple shares a bottle of red wine. Next table over: a man takes a long pull off a glistening glass of pilsner. As I fork into my lasagna, I note the woman in the corner has ordered her second glass of white. Mark notices me staring. "You doing OK?"

"Yeah. It's just that everybody in here is drinking." Not true, but it felt that way.

"We can get our food to go," Mark says, taking a sip of his iced tea.

"No, I'm alright. It's just weird."

I'm not exactly craving a drink, the panicky sensation of a hole that needs to be filled right away. It's more like I have a heightened sense of the drinking going on around me. A hyperawareness that ebbs and flows throughout my first year of sobriety then fades over time. Even today, should a waitress pass by, her tray laden with cocktails, my attention can be momentarily hijacked, an old synapse firing. I've learned that these urges are my disease's way of saying, "Howdy! Still here!" And if I "think the drink" all the way to its known conclusion (me, in the shithouse, full of remorse), the urges will lose their power—and they do.

Chapter Twenty-Three

Mark and I sit on the deck each morning, drinking coffee, smoking, and reading passages from one of his daily reflection books. Then, we join hands and each say a prayer out loud.

"God, keep Melissa safe today," Mark intones, his eyes shut. I peek out of one eye. He looks so earnest, his head bowed as birds chatter in the trees. I can't escape the feeling that what we're doing here is more than a little silly. *Will his prayer actually keep me safe? As if some Grand Chess Master in the sky will be swayed to maneuver his chess pieces to my advantage?* Part of me thinks: *Ridiculous.* Another part: *Please let it be so.*

One evening, I come home from work to discover Mark has turned Sam's old bedroom into a meditation room. He draped a piece of fabric over a small table and set a candle on top. He's placed two beach chairs on either side. Step 11 reads, "*Sought through prayer and meditation to improve our conscious contact with God as we understand Him, praying only for knowledge of His will for us and the power to carry that out.*"

Apparently, that's what we're going to do.

Margaret has given me a book on how to meditate. I've taken a few stabs at it, but it's impossible trying to quiet my monkey mind. Not quite water torture, but close. We go into Sam's room. Mark turns the light off, strikes a match, and lights the candle. We sit in our chairs, encircled by the flame's glow. He sets five minutes on his cell phone alarm. I've told him that's all I can stand. I close my eyes, try to focus on my breathing, and pull my mind back to it when it drifts. The room feels close and warm. I can hear the faucet drip in Sam's bathroom. And then we sit. And sit. My nose itches. Should I scratch it? Will it go away if I don't? But if I don't scratch it, will the itch distract me from meditating? I scratch it. Two seconds later, my elbow itches. I steal a glance at Mark.

He looks like a monk, his face immobile. *Christ, let this be over, so I can go have a cigarette and a cup of decaf on the deck.* My knee itches. Finally, the phone makes a New Age-y harp sound.

"Wow, that was nice," Mark says, rubbing his eyes.

"Yeah, totally groovy," I half-mock.

"You didn't like it?"

Back in the kitchen, I put the kettle on the stove for coffee. "I just can't settle my mind. It's impossible. And I can't stop itching. Do you itch?"

"Not really. I think you just have to ignore those sensations, and they go away. Meditating is like anything else; it takes practice." I point the coffee spoon at him.

"You didn't seem to have a problem."

"Meditation is like a muscle: you have to use it for it to get stronger." When did he become such an expert?

A few days later, when I get home from work, Mark calls me into Sam's room. "This is called a God Box," he says, pointing to an old FedEx box. "I learned about this in one of my meetings. You write whatever's troubling you on a piece of paper and put it in here." He points to a slit he's cut in the top of the box. "The idea is to let go of the worry. Let God take care of it."

"Great," I say, thinking, *Are we going to become one of those couples who trudge through neighborhoods, knocking on doors dressed in their Sunday finery, urging homeowners to embrace the Lord?* I never put a slip bearing my troubles in the God Box. I don't think Mark does either.

Eventually, it disappears from the table. After a handful of times, we stop meditating together.

*   *   *

My early weeks of sobriety are marked by what feels like a kind of spiritual bipolar disorder. Almost every weekday at noon, I jump in my car and make the twenty-minute trip to a meeting group on the northwest side of town, where most members are professional types. Some days, I sit in the meeting and feel like an imposter. Other days, a growing gratitude swoops down and thumps me on the head. I can't recall which morning it is, but early on, perhaps a month after rehab, as I sit in my car at a stoplight, the realization hits: I'm not drinking. *And it's not sucking.* To the contrary, the urge to drink is being supplanted by something new, a sensation that feels something like...contentment. I grab the steering wheel and shout, "Thank you, thank you, thank you!" I couldn't tell you for sure who, or what, I was thanking. But by that point, it seemed immaterial. Something was working.

As days pass, 12-Step speak seeps further into our household lingo. Steeped as we are in our respective recoveries, Mark and I walk around the house spouting program talk, sometimes making a joke of it, as is our tendency. I say something snide or sarcastic to Mark, and he glibly replies, "Sounds like someone needs a meeting." He criticizes something I do, and I rejoin, "Quit taking my inventory."

Perhaps in reaction to the spine I am slowly growing, bone molecule by bone molecule, my husband starts to find lots to criticize about me. First on the list: my continued smoking, even though he reluctantly joins me every night on the deck for coffee and a cigarette, a mirror of our drinking roundelay. ("I can't quit until you quit," he grouses.)

And he's become obsessed with my pigsty of a car, the discarded cups and water bottles on the passenger floorboard, fast-food wrappers, books, and yoga clothes.

We stand in the living room and argue about it. I hold a white trash bag filled with the crap from my floorboard.

"It's my car. Why are you so bent out of shape?"

"Because I have to ride in it sometimes. Plus, it's just not right. You shouldn't let your car get so trashed."

In our decades-long marriage, my car has never been a paragon of cleanliness, a fact that's never bothered him until now. There are other points of conflict. Like many alcoholics in early sobriety, I've developed a thing for sugar. Some nights, I stop by the convenience store on the way home from work and purchase a pint of Ben & Jerry's. Once home, I crank back in my recliner, pop the lid, and devour the whole thing.

"I can't believe you're eating all that," Mark says, watching me lick the spoon. "That can't be healthy."

"Hey, I'm not drinking. Get off my case."

In addition to attending recovery meetings, I'm seeing Joan for therapy. Mark and I are also going to her for marriage counseling. When I tell Joan about Mark carping about my ice cream consumption, I assume she'll take my side. Instead, her face creases.

"You don't want to replace one addiction with another," she says.

Her words scare me enough that I cool it with the Ben & Jerry's, though I still find ways to consume sugar in one form or another. (I will eventually trade the cigarettes for vaping, and then the vaping for plain old air.) But Mark continues to find fault. Since he can't complain about my drinking anymore, he shifts tactics, finding other knives to twist. Turns out, this is not an uncommon scenario in marriages where the drunk gets sober. The non-alcoholic spouse, used to being in the driver's seat, starts to flail around, having lost their favorite weapon of admonishment: control.

Joan and I continue to plumb my poor self-concept, my tendency to obsess over what others think of me. Part of 12-Step recovery involves exploring negative patterns of thought and behavior that cause pain and can lead one back to the bottle. The Steps call them "character defects" or "shortcomings," words that have always rung a bit judgmental to me, reminiscent of outdated ideas that alcoholics were simply weak and morally flawed. But I can hang with negative patterns of thought and behavior.

Words matter.

Per her instructions, I stand before the bathroom mirror each morning and chant positive affirmations, sounding like one of those old *Saturday Night Live* Stuart Smalley skits: "I'm good enough, I'm smart enough, and, doggone it, people like me!" It feels so stupid that I stop after a few days. Eventually, I come upon the work of Brené Brown and Kristin Neff, two researchers who've made a study out of human shame and self-compassion, respectively. Their core ideas—that no one is good enough or smart enough or likable enough all the time *and that's OK*—prove revelatory.

Margaret is a big fan of Thomas Merton, a Trappist monk who wrote books on spiritual growth. Merton believed such growth entails a letting go of the constructed identities that result from wounds experienced in childhood. You must relinquish these masks to move toward authenticity, he believed.

It was a desire I uttered early on in my meetings with Margaret, before she'd even brought up Merton: I want to be authentic.

Such growth entails a "series of humiliations to the false self," Merton taught.

As the weeks and months unspool, I suffer a series of such humiliations, so many it starts to feel like the universe is hitting me over the head with a cosmic two-by-four. These assaults seem to carry within them a singular message: Get over feeling bad about yourself. Get over yourself, period.

Some of these incidents are small, barely mentionable, but deliver a cumulative impact. Others feel huge and pack an immediate wallop.

Let's start with Kevin.

Kevin is the hot-shot investigative reporter who sits directly opposite me in our work cubicle. We're practically in each other's laps. He's trim, with the agile look of a fox. Kevin is the undisputed star of the newsroom. He's funny but on the taciturn side. At least with me, anyway. He talks to his other pod-mates—all of them younger than me and way hipper—but it's as if I'm invisible. When he arrives in the morning, he never meets my eyes. Should I venture a "Good morning," the most I get in return is a barely audible "Hey." There could be only one reason for our chilly discourse: Kevin hates me. Not only does he hate me, but he possesses a sixth sense that picks up on some quirk in my character so twisted he can't stomach even looking at me. On the rare occasion he actually says something to me, I'm wound so tight I come off as either a lunatic or a half-wit.

It's the day after Thanksgiving. The newsroom is a ghost town, with clusters of dark computer screens. Even the jumbo TVs near the printers are turned off. We're a skeleton crew, as many employees have taken the day off. I get in early, looking forward to a quiet day of work. Or, really, just wasting time, which for me consists of reading online sites like *Salon, Slate, the New York Times*, and other newspapers. After a while, Kevin saunters in, along with another young male reporter who sits several cubicles over. Kevin sits down, drops his satchel, and taps on his computer without acknowledging my existence. After a moment or two, he twists in his seat away from me, all but yelling to the young reporter across the way: "Hey Daniel, who is going to edit us today if we write something?"

The question lands like a slap on my face. Kevin didn't ask me who is going to edit us today. He felt the need to turn away and yell the question halfway across the newsroom. There can be only one explanation: he thinks I don't write enough stories. He's right, I'm lazy. I don't write enough stories. I deserve to be fired. Surely everyone in the newsroom thinks I'm a burnout who doesn't carry her own weight. I get up from my desk, hurry down the linoleum aisle, pass the mail slots, and push into the women's room. It's empty, but I check each individual stall to make sure I'm alone. Then I go into my favorite stall, the one nearest to the door. I carefully lock the latch. If any of my coworkers could see what I'm about to do, they'd think me an absolute fool. I am an absolute fool. Please God, let there not be any hidden cameras in the ladies' restroom. I drop to my knees, lean my forearms on either side of the porcelain seat, and rest my butt on my winter boots. The water below is shimmery and clear, reflecting the visage of an absurd woman who has been reduced to praying above a toilet. I close my eyes.

"Please, God, help me not care if Kevin likes me. Please cure me of my obsession with what other people think about me. Help me stop worrying that I'm a pariah among my cooler, smarter, hipper colleagues. Help me to just not give a damn. Help me to realize that not everyone is going to like me, and that's perfectly OK, because not everyone is my cup of tea. Amen."

I stand up, wash my hands at the sink—*talk about an unhygienic prayer*—avoiding looking in the mirror. Me and my absurd gumball theology—as if the Creator of the Universe could be bothered to listen to a self-obsessed woman crouched over a commode, a big 'ole baby worried her co-workers don't like her. Meanwhile, throughout the Third

World, millions of children succumb to dysentery. I should be ashamed of myself.

I sit back down in front of my computer, careful not to look at Kevin, and return to the website I was perusing before my little meltdown. Having already exhausted my usual supply of online fuck-offery, I had landed on the *San Francisco Chronicle* webpage, a paper I never read. I randomly click on an icon for one of their female columnists, a writer I've never read before (or since). I start reading. The column is about how her elementary school-age daughter is having a hard time fitting in at school. Some popular girls are excluding her. (My eyes start to grow wide.) She's taking it personally, believing this public shunning indicates something is wrong with her. (I sit up straight in my chair.) The columnist goes on to write that she told her daughter that chasing after the approval of others is a no-win game. Then I come to this sentence: "One element of growing up and becoming mature is realizing that not everyone is going to like you." I look up from the computer, blink a few times. *For real?* What are the odds my workplace restroom prayer about not being liked would be immediately followed by relevant online counsel, plucked from the cyber-ether, that being liked by everyone isn't important? That growing up means letting go of that goal? Did God answer my prayer? Or was I once again deciphering a pattern in what was, in reality, mere randomness?

All I know is this: that afternoon marked the start of a slow process that took place over my first year of sobriety, a gradual loosening of my enslavement to the approval of others. Not a total break. It's only human to want to be accepted by the clan, an evolutionary impulse that began when our hominid ancestors left the trees and formed tight clumps, lowering the risk of getting eaten on the savannah. Like addiction, the need for approval dwells in the primitive part of the brain. Still, from that day forward, my obsession with what others think of me slowly begins to diminish, as if someone were turning down the heat on a thermostat.

I'm an alcoholic, so I overdo things.

Occasionally, I would petition the church of gumball theology a little too often. When a series of prescribed medicines didn't fix a clogged ear, I got down on my knees in the den one evening and summarily asked God to cure me. Nothing happened. Over time, the ear unclogged on its own. The divine message, I think: fix your own goddamn ear.

I knew my obsession with Kevin was on its way out when I had a strange dream about him. It was a week or two after the bathroom stall prayer. Upon awakening, I sat up in bed and thought: *Whoa*. Then I started laughing. The dream, while not explicit, carried frank erotic undertones. Kevin was a handsome guy, but I had zero romantic designs on him, being married and decades older, to boot. I called Margaret while driving home from work that day.

"You're not going to believe this," I said. "I had a sex dream about Kevin."

She erupted into hoots of laughter. Margaret knew all about the fear that my cubicle mate hated me.

"Oh my God!" she squealed. "What do you think it means?" I glanced into the rearview mirror, then deftly changed lanes.

"I think it's my Higher Power telling me to lighten the fuck up."

According to the program, this is a cardinal issue with most alcoholics: a self-centeredness that places their own needs and desires at the core of everything. Frankly, I think it's the cardinal issue of most human beings. Alcoholics just find alcohol to be the perfect, if fleeting, solution.

I'll soon learn the wonderful Eleanor Roosevelt quote that sums up the whole issue rather poetically: "You wouldn't worry so much about what others think of you if you realized how seldom they do."

Kevin, by the way, seems to warm to me over time once I chill out about whether he likes me or not. An inveterate prankster, he'll sometimes creep up behind my desk during Fiesta to crack a confetti-filled cascarone egg over my head. Then there's the fake cockroach he sometimes leaves on my computer keyboard, causing me to all but jump out of my chair.

I scream and feign melodramatic outrage at these indignities, but of course, I love every minute of it.

Chapter Twenty-Four

I'm still a non-drinker living in a drinking world.

Mark and I attend a gala, courtesy of an invitation from my mother. Galas were always great occasions for me to get looped pre-sobriety. On this night, we belly up to the bar and order Diet Cokes. I circle the silent auction table. Everything is bright and sharp and full of detail. *Oh, look at that woman in the mink. She and her husband are drinking martinis. Interesting choice.* After an hour, Mark and I are herded with the others into the ballroom, where we sit at a large round table with strangers. After dinner, waiters began circulating with bottles of champagne. I'd done just fine during the meal, making small talk with my table mates, slicing bites of tenderloin. But then it comes time for the champagne toast. I hoist my tea glass, take a sip. Everything is OK. Then one waiter, a chubby guy stuffed into his black-and-white penguin suit, approaches me. Ma'am, wouldn't you like some champagne? I smile. "Oh, no thank you." A few minutes pass. Again, he approaches. Now, some champagne? Again, I smile. No. I said no. More minutes pass. Here he comes once more. It's like this asshole has a magnet buried in his sausage-shaped body, drawing him to me again and again. A third time he approaches, bottle held aloft, the question on his face:

Champagne?

I glare at him, shake my head. I'm about to scream that I DON'T WANT ANY *FUCKING* CHAMPAGNE!

He finally skulks away.

The holidays arrive. I'm about three months sober. I tell my family it's fine if they want to have alcohol at Thanksgiving, something we've always done. My sister is insistent: No booze. Her dictum bothers me. Why won't she listen to me? On Turkey Day, I wander into the kitchen and spy my brother-in-law pouring beer into a jumbo convenience store cup, then fixing the lid and a straw. I pretend I don't see him.

Was he doing this for my benefit or to hide his own drinking?

Soon, Christmas commercials appear on TV, the stores fill with holiday shoppers. Wood smoke scents the chilly air. We go to a Christmas party at a mansion owned by a man whose company is a big donor to Mark's non-profit. His son is a photographer; the party is doubling as his art show. Glasses of Diet Coke in hand, we mingle with the well-heeled guests, admiring the photos. At one point, we stand around the buffet table, chatting with a couple we know from our old church. I step toward a nearby cut-crystal punch bowl, wanting something else to drink.

"I don't believe that has alcohol in it," the wife assures me *sotto voce*, as if this information needs to be kept under wraps. So, word has spread to my old congregation that I'm a drunk.

As we walk to our car after the Christmas party, Mark lets out a big breath.

"Man, that was harder than I thought it would be," he says. "I didn't realize how much a drink or two helped me with some of the anxiety of being at a party. It really helps me relax and have fun."

Interesting, I think.

*　　　*　　　*

Margaret and I do my fifth step in the uninhabited smoker's room at Club 12, the white tendrils from our cigarettes curl up as I vomit out all my fears and resentments over the course of three hours. "Forgiving is not the same thing as forgetting," Margaret says. "It's a process, not a single act, one that doesn't require an apology from the offender. It's something you do for yourself, to free up the psychic headspace you've been giving to people who've hurt you. People who acted out of their own spiritual sickness, their own pain. Their own wounds."

When I'm finally done, clean as an emptied husk, Margaret gives me a long embrace and says, "All your life, you've been searching to find a place to belong, for a sense of acceptance. You've found it now; you're home. In this fellowship. You don't have to look anymore." Tears spring to my eyes because I know she's right. I drive home with a springy elastic feeling inside, the sense of being born anew. I stand in our den, eating a Weight Watchers ice cream bar, telling Mark about our session. Maybe I'm bragging a little.

"Man, I want something like that to happen to me," he says from his recliner.

Ah-ha, I think. For once, I'm beating Mr. Spirituality at his own game. Not a very spiritual thought, though, especially on the heels of a spiritual awakening.

Indeed, I start to see that relinquishing my ego (also known as taking my hands off the wheel, trusting my Higher Power, etc.—all central tenets of 12-Step philosophy) is going to be particularly hard for me.

It's a Saturday night. Mark and I are getting ready to go to a party, where there will be some old friends who work at Planned Parenthood. I'm hyped because I have a story running on the front page the next day about crisis pregnancy centers, places that masquerade as medical clinics but are actually fronts for the anti-abortion industry. I can't wait to tell my Planned Parenthood friends at the party about the exposé, to bask in their praise for my hard work (humbly, of course). Before we head out the door, I call the editor on duty to see if she has any questions. Usually, there is a flurry of last-minute calls before a big story runs. I'm worried I haven't gotten any yet.

"The story is being held," she says. "David has some questions about it."

I thank her politely and hang up. Then I storm into my bedroom and start throwing shoes into my closet, thwacking them against the back wall.

"This fucking pisses me off!" I shout.

Mark stands next to the bed, staring at me. "Why didn't he call me? Why didn't someone tell me it was being held? What about simple goddamn professional courtesy? I could have answered his stupid questions!"

I take a few deep breaths. I know what I have to do. I call Margaret.

"I don't know why he didn't tell me," I say. "I'm so mad."

I don't tell her the real reason for my ire: my puffed-up ego has been denied the opportunity to crow about my story at the party. This is hard to admit, even to myself. Margaret listens.

"I thought I was doing so great in recovery. I guess I haven't quite mastered the whole life-on-life's-terms thing yet."

"Melissa," she says drolly, "you're ninety days sober. You're not Gandhi just yet."

I laugh. She's right, of course. These sorts of mini incidents come along to build muscle, Margaret says, so we can better deal with major incidents that happen in sobriety. Of course, this being a 12-Step program, there's an acronym for it called AFGO—it stands for Another Fucking Growth Opportunity.

Driving to the party, I look out my window at the darkening sky, and yet another realization hits: I actually cared about something I'd written. It's a feeling that had all but disappeared in my final years of drinking.

It turns out that the story had several major errors in it. If it had run that Sunday, we'd have had to publish a major correction.

*   *   *

When I'm a little more than three months sober, Mark has a work assignment that takes him to New York for a week. The second night he's gone, I visit the grocery store. As I push my cart past the wine aisle, my old haunt, a thought bubble appears and hovers: *No one would ever know—no one except me.* Then I picture having to call Margaret, confess my relapse. I continue pushing my cart.

The Sunday after Mark returns home, we attend the speaker meeting at Club 12, which would become our de facto church. Each Sunday, recovered alcoholics recount their stories of redemption, tales that, in their unvarnished power, seem more authentic than anything I'd heard in the stained-glass cathedrals of any organized religion. After the meeting, we stop at a coffee shop for lunch. Midway through, Mark sets his hamburger down on his plate.

"I've had an epiphany," he says. "I think I might be an alcoholic too. I've been in a kind of discomfort ever since you went to rehab."

I put down my forkful of cottage cheese and try to keep my voice measured.

"One thing they say is that alcoholics experience a phenomenon of craving, once they put any amount of alcohol in their body," I say. "It's a feeling of 'One is so good, let's have another.' Can you relate to that feeling?"

"Sometimes. I think."

"Did you drink when you were in New York?"

"Just a Guinness or two." He pauses again. "I just can't imagine my life without any alcohol."

All those times Mark got angry over my drinking, only to end up drinking with me, flashed through my mind.

Perhaps he enabled me all those years because he has a problem, too? I need to tread carefully.

"I can't tell you how to work your program. I can only work my program."

Two days later, Mark says it's no big deal; he can drink a beer or two every now and then. I don't say anything. Time passes, and again he swears off alcohol forever. Mark seems to be stuck on the same teeter-totter I rode when I was drinking, only now I'm the one getting the case of whiplash.

The next day, we call the couple we used to drink heavily with to see if they're available for dinner at a restaurant. They say yes. I make reservations at a neighborhood bistro. Two nights before the date, Mark and I are in bed, reading. I broach the topic tenderly.

"So, will you be drinking at the restaurant?" Mark puts his book down and gives me a studiously bland look.

"You say you aren't bothered by being around alcohol anymore, so it won't bother you if I have a couple of drinks with them." My blood pressure starts to rise.

"I'm asking you to please not drink," I say. "It will make it really hard for me, to be the only one not drinking at the table."

Then Mark drops his bombshell. "I talked to my sponsor about this. He said that for you to ask me not to drink around you is controlling behavior. You're having an expectation."

He's just whipped out a tool from the recovery toolbox—expectations are just resentments under construction. Only here, it feels weaponized.

I don't know how to respond. Wordlessly, I slide out of bed, pad down the hallway, and cross the house to the other bathroom. I close the door, flip on the light, and sit on the toilet. It's close to eleven p.m. Too late to call Margaret. But I need some help. I need backup. I need to know if I'm being unreasonable. I take a breath and punch in her number. She picks up on the second ring. "No, sweetie, it's not too late to call. What's going on?" I pour it out. "It's so unfair," I croak. "Why can't my husband not drink out of solidarity with his newly sober wife?"

"It's not like you're going to a party where everyone is eating peanuts but you," Margaret muses. "It's more serious than that. So, no, I don't think you're being unreasonable."

She tells me to pray, to find the right words to explain how I feel. We hang up. I say a quick prayer: *God, what should I say?* I walk back to the bedroom and slide into bed, feeling calmer.

"What did you just do?" Mark asks.

"I called Margaret."

He lies there quietly for a second or two. Then he rallies with his other line of defense.

"Listen, I'm worried they'll feel weird if I don't drink," he says, referencing our couple friends.

"I see," I said. *What total horse shit.*

"There are three options here," he says, holding up his fingers. "I drink, I don't drink, or we just don't go."

"Then I guess let's just not go," I say. Mark gets a funny look on his face: he wasn't expecting this response. I turn off the light, turn over on my side. After a while, Mark grabs my hand.

"I'm sorry I upset you so much that you had to call your sponsor." Pause.

"Okay, I won't drink," he says.

"Thanks," I say. Inside, I am victorious. *I won! Yippee!*

On the night of the dinner, we meet the other couple at the restaurant. The husband and wife seem subdued. I get the sense I've violated some oath, voluntarily ejected myself from the world of drinkers, and am now an outsider, not to be trusted. Or it could just be my paranoia. The waiter comes to our table.

"I'll have a double Dewar's on the rocks," Mark says. I grab the strap of my purse. Then he says, "Just kidding. I'd like a water with lemon."

The couple doesn't seem to know how to react to this: Is he being humorous? No one says anything. The conversation resumes, this weird little moment going unremarked upon. They order cocktails. At dinner, I consciously try to act like my old drinking self, laughing too much, telling dirty jokes, and dropping the F-bomb. I don't want them to think I've turned into a wet blanket. (Later, Joan will observe, "You didn't want them to think you've changed? But you have changed, haven't you?")

The wife drinks only one glass of white wine with dinner. I know she's holding herself back. I want to say, "Go ahead, drink as much as you want, I won't wonder if you're an alcoholic like me." But I don't say anything.

The uncomfortable meal finally ends.

"Well, that was different," Mark says, putting the car into gear.

"Yeah, they seemed kind of quiet. How did you do?" He swivels his head around.

"What do you mean?"

"Without drinking. How did you do?"

"I did fine." The question seems to annoy him. "What do you mean, 'How did I do?' I did fine. I don't have to drink to have a good time."

My after-care group with Dr. B. is made up of fellow Starlite graduates. I vent my frustration over Mark's decision to continue to drink. He suggests we come in for another couple's session. Back we go on the leather couch. Dr. B listens as Mark explains why he should be able to tipple. The doctor has an amused expression on his face. "I guess I'm wondering why it seems so hard for you to give it up," he says.

"I just don't think I should have to," Mark says. "I'm not an alcoholic, but I enjoy a drink now and then, and I should be allowed to."

Dr. B. says it might be "a good idea" if he didn't drink around me for one year. "After that, you do whatever you want," he says. Mark seems to acquiesce. When I tell Margaret about Dr. B's suggestion, she says it was her ex-husband's drinking that led her to relapse.

I feel vindicated. Everyone is on the same page about Mark's drinking. Great. *Good.* But the next night, as I pull into our driveway after work, my cell phone chirps. It's Margaret.

"I want to read something to you from the Big Book," she says. It's a passage that says an alcoholic's sobriety is between her and her Higher Power. No one else. Not her spouse. Margaret finishes reading, then homes in for the punch.

"When you talk about Mark's drinking, I hear resentment in your voice," she says.

"Oh. Really?" Sitting there in the dark, I picture Margaret's bullshit-detector look.

"This is something you really need to think about."

"Will do, sponsor."

I climb out of the car, miffed. *Doesn't she realize how hard it is to be married to someone who drinks?* I've briefly discussed Mark's drinking with Joan, but she hasn't ruled one way or the other. Instead, she's asked me to look at my motivation. Am I trying to punish Mark since I can't drink?

I think but don't say, *I'm only five months sober. Mark should* want *to abstain.*

For a day or two, I do a slow burn. Then we get invited to a Roman Holiday dinner party. It's one of those game-box parties where everyone dresses in costume and tries to solve a murder mystery. We went to a similar party at the same couple's home about a year ago: the wine flowed as the game went on for hours. I tell Mark that if he plans on drinking at the party, I won't attend.

"All I can do is take care of my own needs," I say, an imperial lift to my chin.

One night during the week before the party, Mark goes out to dinner with donors and comes home smelling like a vineyard. He lies next to me in bed, emanating. I don't say anything. The next evening, he comes home after an individual session with Joan. The minute he walks in the door, I can tell he's loaded for bear.

"Joan said your sobriety is between you and God, not between me and you. You have to deal with it. It's not my job." Dr. B's idea for him to abstain from drinking for a year now strikes him as "unhealthy."

Mark's little speech echoes word-for-word what Margaret said to me in the driveway. Did Margaret share her Big Book lesson with Joan? Joan didn't give the whole it's-between-you-and-God spiel when we discussed Mark's drinking. I feel ganged up on: Are my sponsor, husband, and therapist all in cahoots? Does *no one* care about my fragile sobriety?

If this were the Victorian Age, I'd be melodramatically supine on my fainting couch, the back of one hand on my forehead.

My eyes shoot daggers at Mark.

"Did you talk to Margaret? Because that's what she said," I say. "What's going on here? Is this some sort of group decision?"

"I don't know anything about that. I just know I'm not an alcoholic, so it's not fair for you to expect me to give up something I enjoy and that doesn't hurt me."

"*Whatever.*"

I don't sleep much that night, spending the hours tossing and turning, building an elaborate mental defense.

The next morning, an ice storm blows in. The highways are slick with danger. I have to drive thirty miles per hour into work, gripping the steering wheel. Once there, I compose an email to Joan, copying Mark. It is thick with venom and accusation, a masterwork of hyperbole. I accuse the three of them of collaborating against me, adrenaline zipping through my limbs as I type each word. A little thrill of victory erupts when I hit send. I've said my piece.

No one's going to shut me up anymore.

I drive to Club 12 for a mid-morning meeting, my car sliding when it hits a patch of ice. As I negotiate the road, my mind revisits the email. I'm swelled with righteous indignation. Swinging into a parking space, I think: *My life has done a complete 180 since I left rehab. If Mark thinks we're going to go on as before, hanging out with hard-boozing friends, going to dinner parties where everyone gets sloshed except me—well, the motherfucker's got another thing coming. Maybe I should divorce him. Maybe I should marry someone in the program. There's that cute, stocky guy with the earring in my home group who's always smiling at me.*

Right before I sit down for the meeting, Mark calls. He's read my email.

"I wish you'd talked to me before sending it to Joan."

"Too late." *Ha-ha*, I think. He's been caught out and doesn't like it.

"You're overthinking things," he says.

"I'm just taking care of myself. Too bad you can't understand that. My meeting's starting. I have to go."

I hang up. Later that day, I get on my knees at home, asking God for a way out of this mess. Nothing happens. Then, an email from Joan drops into my inbox. It's measured and thoughtful and completely devoid of ire. She references a particularly self-pitying passage where I write that no one seems to care how Mark's drinking could affect me: "Will there come a time when we can hang out with our drinking friends and Mark can quaff right along with them to his heart's content while I sip a Diet Pepsi? Maybe. Possibly. But not right now. I know that for sure."

Joan's response: "There's so much anger in this statement...It's not Mark's job to take care of you. This is the old dance you two were doing, where you drank too much and Mark took care of you. Now you want the same in your sobriety. Maybe this is an old issue for you."

Then she asks me this, "Who do you wish had taken care of you when you were little?"

That's an easy one. I wished my mother had shielded us from our father's violence, but she largely failed. After he left, she became violent herself, though in a lesser form. The whippings, the spankings, the yelling... that darkened, menacing face. In short, no one protected *me*, not really. Could this whole thing just be a ghost from my past?

There's a saying in recovery: *When you're hysterical, it's historical.*

I go out onto the deck and smoke a cigarette. It's warmed up considerably, the sun shining through puffy winter clouds. Melting ice makes soft, pitter-pat sounds as it drips from the tree branches. The air has a freshly-washed smell. I remove my jacket, re-read my email, and then Joan's response. With the perspective gained by a few hours, my screed is starting to sound pretty childish. I'd left a message for Margaret to call, saying there's something I need to read to her. Now I'm gripped with apprehension. I've essentially accused her of conspiring against me. She may completely lose it and fire me as a sponsee. My phone rings. It's Margaret.

"Hey, the Divine Miss M! What's up?"

With a halting voice, I read her my email, then Joan's response. When I'm finished, I steel myself for her fury. I may look like a grown woman sitting on a deck, but inside I'm a little girl who has broken a rule, standing before a frightening mother. But when Margaret speaks, her voice is calm. Loving, even.

"Let's unpack this," she says. "What are you afraid is going to happen if you go to the Roman Holiday party and Mark drinks?"

"I'm going to feel the rage I felt five years ago, when I quit drinking and we'd go to parties and everyone would get sloshed but me, and I'd want to rip the flesh off their faces."

"Okay. What's different between that time and now?"

I pause. "I know down in my bones that I'm an alcoholic and can't drink."

"That's a pretty big difference."

"Yes, it is."

"The program we're in is about freedom. It's about being able to do anything we want, go anywhere we want, as long as we're in good spiritual condition. You're in a completely different place than you were five years ago. You have knowledge about yourself you didn't have then. So, go to the party. Forget about whether or not Mark drinks. Take your own car. Just stick your toe in the pool. If you find you can't handle it, just leave.

But you won't know how free you can be until you take the risk and try it. I think you're going to be in for a surprise."

I'm silent for a beat or two.

"I guess I could try it. I mean, what am I so afraid of? I'm different now. I'm stronger."

When Margaret speaks next, her voice takes on the sort of resplendent timbre it acquires whenever the spirit is flowing through her.

"You're an empowered woman," she says. "When you were younger and couldn't have orgasms, you went to see a therapist and figured it out. Most women would have suffered in silence. When I look at you, I see a strong woman who is becoming stronger every day. Do not be afraid."

I hang up, feeling juiced. *Truly, what am I afraid of? Why do I have to be afraid of anything?* The day is ending in an entirely different place from where it began.

"Drink if you want at the Roman Holiday party," I tell Mark when he gets home. "Do whatever you want. Really, I'm fine with it."

He gives me a quizzical look. Now he's the one with the whiplash.

"But what about all that stuff you said in your email?"

"Just disregard it. I'm sorry. Just forget about it. Margaret and I talked it out, everything is fine."

"I'm not going to get drunk."

"Mark, I don't care. Do whatever you want to do. It's not my business."

The night of the party, Mark swathes himself in a large white sheet and places a crown of fake grape leaves atop his head. He makes a fine emperor with his perfect Roman nose. I dress in a shimmering Egyptian gown my mother bought on one of her overseas trips. It comes complete with a beaded headdress.

"Are you sure you want to take your own car?" Mark asks in the driveway.

"I'm sure," I say, slipping behind the wheel.

"It seems like a waste of gas," he says.

"Why don't you just let me do my thing, and you do your thing?" I say, leaning my bejeweled head out the window.

Before the game starts, the guests admire each other's outfits. There are three other couples, including the hard-drinking couple, who would end up dropping us as friends after my sobriety sticks. Everyone attends our former church; we've all been social acquaintances for a time. I'm pretty sure everyone knows I've been to rehab, including the hostess. As we settle into couches in the living room, she hands out large crystal goblets of wine and bacon-wrapped figs. I hand her my two cans of Diet Coke.

"Oh, do you want this in a goblet?" she asks loudly, in front of the other couples. "Surely, you want a goblet like everyone else?" Something I'll discover in sobriety: non-alcoholics tend to presume recovered alcoholics fetishize booze-related glassware.

"Sure, a goblet is fine."

We sit in the living room, with its silver brocade curtains, mahogany furniture, and family portraits on the walls. We go through two rounds of cocktails so that everyone can get some ethanol in their blood before dinner and the game begins. I make a point of laughing often. I watch as people sip their goblets of wine. I can smell it—a sense memory floods in, the round feel of wine in my mouth, a déjà vu reminder of how those sips served to sand down the prickles of anxiety I get in social situations. I don't get to have that now. I'm flying solo. Do I want the wine? Sort of. Would I in a million years actually drink any? No. Never. Somehow, on this night, I know this to be true, right down to the soles of my feet.

We move into the dining room and start playing the game. Things are going well. The conversation is diamond-sharp and witty. Hilarious, in fact. I forget about the goblets of wine. We're rocking along through the salad course. Then, midway through the braised pork, it's like a switch gets flipped. My dinner companions, so sparkling and clever, start to turn sophomoric. As the hostess circles the table, refilling wine glasses, it's like everyone has become part barn-animal, guffawing and whinnying and snorting at jokes that aren't funny. Up to now, we've competed to see who can make the cleverest comment about clues to who did the murder. By the time dessert arrives, the collective IQ of the table has sunk to around third-grade level. One guy cackles so hard a big vein bulges on his forehead. His wife, sitting across the table, subtly slides his glass of wine over to her side.

For the first time, I'm on the outside looking in, and I come to a singular, if sanctimonious, observation: *Drunk people are sort of stupid.* The game drones on for more than two hours. I'm dying to leave, not because I want to drink, but because I'm horrendously bored. But I can't leave because it would screw up the game. Finally, the whodunit is solved, although at this point, nobody really cares who the murderer is. I bid goodnight to the revelers, now starting on their night caps. *Adieu, everyone! Early morning tomorrow!* Mark stares quizzically as I traipse out the door.

I suck down two cigarettes in a row on the drive home through darkened streets. I exult. *I survived the gauntlet! For four hours, I sat amidst people getting smashed and didn't want to tear the flesh off anyone's face!* I'm still an alcoholic, I still can't drink, and I'm fine with it. Actually, more than fine. To be honest, I'm feeling a smidge superior, collateral arrogance I know I'll have to confess to Margaret in the morning. No one at the party, to my knowledge, is an alcoholic: there's nothing wrong with them getting drunk and acting like brain-damaged teenagers. I have no right to feel above them. But I do. Sort of.

Mark arrives home and crawls into bed about a half hour later, reeking of wine.

"I didn't get drunk," he says, pulling up the covers.

"Good," I say, looking up from the book I'm reading. "I'm glad."

We chat about the party, how tasty the food was, how drunk so-and-so got, how we couldn't believe that so-and-so said this-and-that. The typical post-party debriefing that goes on between spouses. I'm careful to stay neutral when Mark brings up how many bottles of wine were consumed. The next day is a Saturday. We're signed up for an all-day seminar at Joan's office on the Enneagram, an ancient system of spiritual direction. Based on a nine-sided geometric figure, it's a tool that is supposed to foster growth by helping you identify where you fall among nine basic personality types. I'm not really buying it, but it seems like a fun way to spend a Saturday morning.

Mark wakes up from his Roman bacchanalia with a hangover.

"I feel like total shit," he says. I turn away so he won't see my self-satisfied smile.

"I overdid it, and it wasn't even that fun."

I just nod and keep my words of wisdom, or *whatever,* to myself.

The Roman Holiday party marked a turning point for me, just as Margaret thought it might. I learned I could be around drinking, even excessive drinking, even *Mark's* drinking, and stay safe in my cocoon of sobriety. According to the Big Book, this meant I'd experienced the "psychic change." It's a psychobabble phrase for a simple idea—getting to a place in recovery where you don't have to fight the urge to drink anymore. You enter a zone of neutrality. The problem has been removed, and it *stays* removed if you follow a few simple actions. Like meetings. Prayer. Spending time with other alcoholics.

There are a handful of occasions over the early years of my sobriety when Mark drinks too much. Usually while in the company of certain male friends who like to over-imbibe. He'll get the tell-tale shit-eating grin that heralds his drunkenness. He'll come up to me, place his palms on either side of my face and croon "Oh, Ba, I love you so much." I remember this gambit—it's the drunk love talk we used to do when we were both wasted. I push his hands away, tell him to cut it out. It bugs me, not so much because I'm hungering to go back to the time in our lives where I'm drunk talking, too. It's because I know his display is inauthentic.

Like my son said at the long-ago family meeting at the intensive outpatient program: I like my husband when he's being who he truly is.

But as the years pass, Mark's consumption naturally starts to dwindle. Turns out, without a drunken wife egging him on, he's basically a one-beer-a-day kind of guy. Getting older also helps.

If Mark had kept drinking heavily, I'm not sure where we would have ended up. Divorce court, probably.

But on the morning after the Roman murder mystery, we're not yet out of the relationship woods—not by a long shot.

The day after the party, Mark swallows some Advil and showers off the residue of his evening in ancient Rome.

We drive to Joan's office, not knowing the Enneagram seminar, so anodyne on its face, will end up almost tearing my marriage apart once again.

Chapter Twenty-Five

The Enneagram workshop takes place in a small conference room next to Joan's office. She and another therapist named Beverly sit at a large round table, greeting participants as we file in and grab a cup of coffee and a doughnut. There are about twenty of us—all clients of Joan and Beverly. Most everyone is in recovery. I recognize a few faces from Club 12. We go around the circle and introduce ourselves, then spend the rest of the morning filling in worksheets geared to help us discern which of the nine basic personality types we are. They're hopelessly dated. Guess which Enneagram type Michael Douglas is! Phyllis Diller! We go around the circle and disclose which number we think we are and the implication it holds for our lives, our recovery, and our relationships with others. It's all pretty silly, but I gamely go along. By the end of the session, I've decided I'm an artist, given my career in writing. Mark decides he's a caretaker.

Innocent, right?

Later in the week, I come home from work and go into the bathroom. While I sit on the toilet, Mark is ironing a shirt in our bedroom. We're attending a gala in an hour to watch a local philanthropist receive an award. I'm writing a profile on him for the newspaper.

"How was your meeting with Joan?" he yells from the bedroom. I'd gone to therapy that day.

"It was good," I yell back. "I told her about that book I'm reading."

The book is *You Can't Make Me Angry*. It's a self-help tome on how to maintain your emotional sobriety, the psychic corollary to physical sobriety. It's a "how-to" on staying on an even keel. At six months sober, I'm still hoovering up books on recovery and spirituality.

"I told her about how you've been getting pretty angry at me lately, for little stuff. Like my messy car." I flush the toilet and walk into the bedroom.

"And do you wonder why I'm angry?" Mark goads, spritzing water on his shirt.

"I don't know. Because I don't measure up to your standards sometimes?"

He readjusts the shirt, presses the iron down on the collar.

"You kept drinking for years even though you knew it made me unhappy. You only got sober when I packed a bag and left you."

My fear antenna from childhood, still exquisitely sensitive, locks into the upright position.

"First of all, you weren't unhappy about my drinking all the time," I say.

"A lot of the time, you were right there drinking with me." No response. The iron slides back and forth.

"Secondly, I was a sick person. Why can't you have compassion for me?"

"I'm not saying I don't have compassion for you. But I'm still angry." There doesn't seem to be much more I can say.

"I guess we'll work it out in Joan's office," I offer.

We drive to the gala in silence. As Mark slides quarters into the parking meter, I feel like I'm going to burst. We have to resolve this discussion before we go into the dinner.

"Listen, I apologize for all the years I drank and made you unhappy. I've already made my formal amends to you, but I will say it again. I'm sorry."

Silence.

"I guess I'm supposed to say something," he says.

"What are you thinking?"

"I keep thinking about Henry, this guy in my program who's also in yours. He's had lots of sponsees relapse, but it was his wife's relapse that he just couldn't get over."

"Are you saying you can't get over the times I relapsed?"

Mark searches his pockets for one last quarter, doesn't respond. I'm starting to get angry. The book I'm reading insists that other people can't make you angry—it's something you allow. Sounds great in theory, but I'm not sure how well it works in the real world. My pulse is beating in my throat.

"You had a role in my drinking," I say. "For those five years when it got bad, we were two people stuck in a sick dynamic. You're not some Mr. Innocent here."

Mark says nothing. We go into the gala and for the next three hours, everything seems fine. Until we get home. When I turn on the kitchen light, the yellow glow illuminates the bottles of olive oil and balsamic vinegar I'd left on the counter from the night before. Mark stomps over, grabs the bottles, and puts them in the pantry.

"We're supposed to be keeping the house clean, and now we're not doing it," he shouts. It's a new rule he instituted upon my return from rehab: a house always neat and tidy.

"I can see you're angry," I say in my best imitation of Joan.

"I'm not angry. I just want to keep the house clean." He puts the bag of coffee in the cupboard. We never keep the coffee in the cupboard. It's always on the counter. Mark goes from room to room, frantically tidying up. I follow along, hectoring him as I go. "Why are you cleaning the house at ten o'clock?"

"What's wrong with that?" he says.

"You're mad because I left the oil and vinegar out. I feel like I'm always walking on eggshells around you these days." He stands up from stacking errant days-old newspapers. He hasn't even taken his tie off yet.

"See! You always say 'always.' Why do you always have to exaggerate?"

"OK, maybe eighty-five percent of the time," I say. Pause. "Didn't you just say I *always* exaggerate?"

"Eggshells, huh? That must be a hard way to live," he says, throwing the newspapers in the recycling bin. "I can't influence how you feel. Only you can do that."

"But I'm impacted by the way you treat me," I say, trailing him down the hall. "I'm starting to realize some things are acceptable and some things aren't."

Mark doesn't respond, so I take out the sharpest arrow from my quiver. The one I know will hit him where it hurts.

"I think you have tons of unexamined anger at your mother. I'm just a convenient target."

Mark pauses in cleaning, stands ramrod straight. Then he takes out his sharpest arrow.

"I feel like I'm stuck in a loveless marriage."

The comment lands like a blow, but I can't let him know he's hit pay dirt.

"I understand what you mean."

"Good. We're both on the same page."

We climb into bed. From experience, I know Mark will slide into sleep within moments, his body slipping the shackles of our fight, while I'll spend the next few hours stewing, mulling over our argument and rehearsing future ones. I only have a brief window. I proceed delicately.

"Dr. B said the other day the real emotion behind anger is actually fear. I'm wondering if something about me being in recovery is making you afraid, and maybe that's why you're so angry at me."

A slight pause. "I guess I have to think about that," he says, his back to me.

I return to my book, read the same sentence over and over again. Mark stirs, says over his shoulder: "Maybe saying it's a loveless marriage was too harsh. But I feel like we're just two ships passing in the night. We never eat meals together. We never have sex."

"I understand."

It feels like another gig. Mark has groused about how my life is now so full of recovery meetings and sessions with Margaret and therapy with Joan that I don't seem to have time for him. Recovering alcoholics are warned about this: the same loved ones who harped about your drinking may start complaining about the time it takes for you to stay sober.

But Mark has a point about the sex: I never initiate. My interest in sex ranks below zero. I realize I've been selfish, ignoring Mark's needs simply because I'm libido-challenged. I make a mental note to see a doctor about this.

In the morning, Mark puts his arm around me before he leaves for work. "We'll work it out," he says, although it doesn't sound convincing.

I try to occupy my mind at work, but the bile keeps rising: Mark is trying to force me back into a child's position, the one I inhabited as a guilt-ridden drunk. But I'm not letting him, and he's not liking it. It almost feels like my husband *wants* me to drink again, if only to restore the familiar power balance of our marriage. This, too, is something we're warned about in recovery. When I get home, he's once again in the bedroom, ironing a shirt.

We're having dinner at a downtown Mexican restaurant, then going to a poetry reading at a local arts organization, where I'm signed up to take a memoir writing class the next day. It's a Friday night. At dinner, Mark seems distant. We crunch on a basket of tortillas chips, not speaking. The diners around us talk, laugh, lean their heads together. I can tell there's something Mark wants to say. He finally says it.

"I've been unhappy in our marriage for a long time," he says. "I thought if you got sober it would fix things, but it hasn't."

The swirl of the restaurant around me falls away. The feeling of desperation that marked my last days of drinking, when Mark decamped to a hotel, rises in my throat. "Do you love me?" It comes out like a squeak. "I'm not sure I know what love is," Mark says.

Almost three decades in a relationship with me and he doesn't know what love is?

Our food arrives. I try to eat, but the cheese enchilada is a glutinous blob in my mouth. I feel trapped in a bad dream, or maybe held under water, as if any moment the pressure will pop and the mariachis will start singing and the restaurant will start moving again and my husband will smile at me from across the table and say don't worry, *I'm just kidding*, I love you, everything is going to be alright. Mark signs the bill.

I have to say something before we leave.

"What is it you want to do?"

"I don't know," he says, his face impassive. *Who is this man?*

"Maybe a separation."

"A separation?"

"Yes. I think I need some time apart from you, to see what I want to do."

The exact words he said when he left over my drinking.

We go to the poetry reading, but I can't pay attention. Mark feels like a stranger sitting next to me. One poet is a young Latino man who flounces through his lyrics, punchy lines that are sly and earthy and of-the-body. After one of his big endings, Mark gives a satisfied grunt. The woman writer who has organized the reading murmurs, *"Oh, yes."* *Maybe this is the problem*, I think. *I'm not a sensual person who can respond in a visceral way to poetry. This is why my husband is going to leave me. He deserves to be with a more sexual woman.*

221

We drive home in silence. In bed, we are continents apart. My skin feels as if it's splitting at the seams. I'm still reading the book on anger. I come to a passage that states a spouse may focus on what their partner is doing wrong as a way to control them. I take a gamble.

"Will you please read this sentence?"

Mark nods, takes the book from my hands. Reads.

"Hmm," he says.

"What am I doing wrong?" I ask.

He puts his hand in mine for a moment. "Not anything," he says.

For the second night in a row, it takes me hours to fall asleep. When I wake in the morning, more tired than when I went to sleep, Mark is gone. He said the night before he was going to help a friend move today. The friend is Trevor, a middle-aged man who has had multiple marriages and struggles in his relationships with women. After I got back from rehab, Mark confessed to me that Trevor had advised him to leave me when I was still drinking. I'd long nurtured the suspicion Trevor was jealous of our relationship. I'd told Mark about this. Now, with our marriage dangling by a thread, he is spending an entire day with this man. Ragged from lack of sleep, I call Margaret. "I need an emergency meeting."

"Tell me what's going on."

I spill out the events and conversation of the preceding two nights.

"I think Mark is threatened by your recovery," Margaret says.

I have to leave for the memoir writing workshop but tell Margaret I will call her later. She advises me to pray, go to a meeting, and realize that early recovery is often marred by such bumps. You will get through it, she promises. The statistic keeps running through my head: *Many marriages where the alcoholic gets sober still end in divorce.*

Before I leave the house, I call Mark.

"I know you're going to talk about what's going on with Trevor, but I would ask you to consider the source when it comes to any advice he might give you."

Mark's anger blooms through the phone line.

"Please don't try to tell me who I can and can't talk to."

In the parking lot before I go into the seminar, I call Margaret from my car. I want to read her a passage in my anger book, which quotes the famous poem about how the universe is unfolding as it should. Perhaps a divorce is simply in the cards for me. I commence boo-hooing.

"Do you think I'm lovable?" I am a pathetic puddle of goo.

"Of course you are," she says, followed by a string of nurturing words that only make me cry harder. *I've got to get a grip*, I tell myself, hanging up.

In the workshop, a dozen people cluster around a wood table. The teacher is engaging and witty, but I hear only half of what he says. I'm a leaf hanging by a filament, ready to blow away in the wind. Can the other students tell I'm a loser about to get left by her spouse? When class is over, I turn the key in the ignition, but instead of an engine rev all I get are clicks. The battery (once again) is dead. I must have been distracted by my conversation with Margaret and not turned the car fully off. I call Mark, but he doesn't answer. I call my mother. No answer. Out of options, I call a cab.

At home, Margaret calls me. As we talk, I pace up and down our front sidewalk, chain smoking, almost wearing a groove in the concrete. For the first time there's a glimmer of anger in her own voice, which strangely heartens me.

"I talked to Dorothy"— Margaret's sponsor— "and she and I both think Mark is playing his trump card. With this separation idea, he's pulling an emotional geographic." (A "geographic" is a term in the program that connotes a drunk's attempt to escape his drinking problem by physically moving.) "He's trying to sabotage you. Maybe get you to drink, who knows," Margaret continues. "You just work your program. Let him deal with whatever he's going through. Dorothy and I both agree that if all this isn't making you want to drink, you've had the psychic change, girl."

It dawns on me: In the past two days I hadn't once thought about taking a drink. Slitting my wrists, maybe. Throwing a rope over the bedroom closet rod. But not opening a wine bottle.

When Mark comes home, he digs in the garage for the jumper cables. He comes into the kitchen, holding the grimy cables in his hands.

"Why didn't you go into the restaurant and ask someone to give you a jump?" he demands.

"I wasn't comfortable with that."

I follow him over to the restaurant. We don't speak as he jumps the car. Back at home, he stretches out in his recliner and takes a nap. I stare at his slack-jawed mouth. I decide to go to a five-thirty meeting at Club 12, which is less crowded during dinner time on a Saturday evening. It's a small group, mostly men. I unload about what's going on at home, even though it's considered bad form to delve too deeply into super-personal matters during meetings. (That's better suited for a talk with your sponsor.) But I let it rip, crying a bit toward the end. The men look at me with understanding in their eyes.

"When it comes to recovery in a marriage, sometimes spouses aren't at the same table at the same time," one man says. "You've just got to put it in God's hands."

I walk out of the meeting feeling ten pounds lighter. At home, we order a pizza and watch an episode of *Breaking Bad*. During an ad break, Mark turns to me.

"What I'm talking about, the separation, doesn't necessarily have to lead to divorce. I was reading about separation. It can be a healthy thing, and a lot of couples get back together afterward."

I put my crust down on my plate, wipe my mouth with a napkin.

"I see."

"This isn't something I'm doing to you, it's something I'm doing for us."

I take a big gulp of iced tea, then do my best once again to channel Joan and Margaret, the voices of rationality.

"You're conflicted in your feelings, but I'm not conflicted in my feelings for you. I'll respect whatever gives you clarity of mind." *Even if it's grade-A hog shit*, I think.

What I don't think about, don't even consider, is the pain and resentment that Mark must still be holding onto, after the five years of agony I put him through, as he helplessly watched me deeply wound our only child. As my drinking and repeated relapsing tore down the ramparts of trust that undergirded our marriage. Now, here I was, the shiny new recovered person, heroic and brave, expecting to be congratulated and coddled at every turn. No wonder he's going crazy. Self-centered in the extreme (the signal trait of alcoholics, or perhaps everyone), I don't fully grasp what Mark is going through.

It drives him crazy when I act needy, I know this. I want to rail at him, shake him, beg him not to leave me. Instead, I sit in my recliner and pretend our possible marital dissolution is no big deal. He's gone all the next day, helping Trevor again. I go to the Sunday morning Club 12 speaker meeting and sit in the smoker's room, eating a bag of vending machine cookies, morosely crunching. I feel like I'm drowning. That evening, Mark calls me from his cell.

"Do you want to go to Simi's and have Indian food?"

"Sure."

I stand by the window in our living room, drink a glass of water and watch for his car to pull up. I rest the water glass on the windowsill. *Okay*, I think. *Whatever you want, I'll do. If I have to debase myself, I'll do it. If I have to say I fucked everything up and I'm wrong and I'm to blame for everything, I'll do it. If I have to apologize for being a drunk every day for the rest of my life, I'll do it. Just don't leave me. Don't leave me like my father did.*

His van pulls up. I wait for him to come in. He doesn't come in. My phone rings again.

"You coming out?"

We study our menus at Simi's. Mark orders a beer. The mask glued to his face all weekend seems to have slipped some, showing signs of the man I know.

"I've had an epiphany," he says. "That Enneagram workshop really revealed something for me."

Oh *fuck*. Another epiphany.

What it revealed, he goes on to say, is that all his life he's been a caretaker, putting other people's needs first. Especially me. Now he's done with all that.

"I'm seeing things with clarity," he says, dipping a samosa in chutney. "I've been worrying obsessively that what I'm going through is going to make you drink, but I can't worry about that anymore. I have to take care of myself."

Okay, I think, *I can work with this. He needs to put his feelings first. Okay, good. Put your feelings first. See if you can do this without leaving me.*

"We'll talk about this more on Wednesday with Joan," I resolve. That night, I sleep well for the first time in days. The next evening, Mark has dinner with a male friend of ours. He and his wife are both in the program.

"I've had an epiphany," he says, walking in the door afterwards. (Jesus Christ.) "This is not the time for me to leave. We need to work together on this."

"That sounds great."

"We've removed the alcohol from our marriage, but I'm still married to an alcoholic."

"Yeah, and I'm still married to an Al-Anon." Tiny gig.

That night we laugh in bed together at *The Daily Show*. It almost feels like things are back to normal. But the next morning, Mark is distant again, barely kissing me goodbye.

"I'm wondering now again if maybe a separation would be a good thing."

"Let's just wait and talk with Joan."

An ember of anger is starting to burn. Part of me wants to tell Mark he can take his epiphanies and *shove them up his ass.*

That afternoon, we sit on opposite sides of Joan's couch. We display our various weapons, shiny and sharp. Mark: She's messy. She doesn't listen to me. She doesn't want to have sex. She's complacent. She's a people-pleaser.

"She's just happy to get up in the morning, have her coffee and cigarette, go to work. Then she comes home, plays with the dog, then gets in her recliner and reads with the TV on."

"You're hardly Mr. Excitement," I say.

Me: He's controlling, full of anger. He's threatened by my sobriety. He's mourning our old drinking life. All this business about my messiness is just a proxy for the fact he can't deal with a sober wife.

"And I've told Mark I'm seeing a doctor about the sex thing."

"That's just so I won't leave you," he says. "You don't really care about sex."

Joan finally speaks up.

"If you don't have any desire for sex, it's hard to care about it if your desire is gone," she says.

Ha! She's on my side! Then Joan turns to me.

"Your messy habits could be passive-aggressive. If being neat matters to a spouse, the other spouse needs to shape up."

On and on. We thrust and parry, each blaming the other for our predicament. When our fifty minutes are up, Joan is surprisingly upbeat.

"I don't know if a long separation is a good idea right now. Maybe a short one. And Melissa, maybe you can take some time alone." I'd never thought of it: maybe I should separate from Mark?

"She's going to be all mad and pouty when I take mine," Mark says.

"That's not your business," Joan says. Then she smiles.

"The fact that you're both here, that you're both in recovery programs, means your marriage has an excellent prognosis."

I wish I could feel as cheery. Joan gives the speech we've both heard before: Each person in a marriage is enclosed by an invisible hula-hoop. Where the hoops intersect in the middle is where intimacy happens. We agree to spend a half hour talking to each other at the end of each day, and to come back in two weeks. I relay the gist of the session to Margaret.

"Complacent? It sounds to me like you're content," she says. "Everything Mark is saying is all *me, me, me*. Have you thought of saying to him, 'You want to leave? Go ahead and leave.'"

That whole week, things stay cool at home. Again, we're in bed at night. I'm reading yet another self-help book. This one is written by John Gottman, the marriage therapist who famously claimed he can tell if a couple is going to make it in under ten minutes. He came up with the "four horsemen of the apocalypse" that can torpedo a relationship: stonewalling, criticism, contempt, and defensiveness. He could be describing my marriage.

"This book is amazing," I say. On the back page, I notice Gottman's organization hosts marriage workshops around the country. I google the website and learn one such event is happening in Dallas the next week.

"This therapist puts on workshops to fix marriages, and there's one in Dallas," I say. "Do you want to go?"

"Only if it addresses alcoholism in a marriage."

Rage suddenly floods me. I slap the book down in my lap.

"You can't blame everything on my drinking! You had a role too. There was a dynamic at work."

He's matter-of-fact, refusing to rise up and take the bait.

"Of course there was. But if a therapist doesn't understand the dynamics of addiction, we're wasting our time."

"I'm sick of this shit. You're blaming everything on me." *An invisible Dr. Gottman sits in the corner, taking notes.*

"You drank for years knowing it made me angry," Mark says. "And before you say it, I know alcoholism is a disease."

His friend John told him sometimes there are too many hurts in a marriage to heal.

"You take me for granted," he says. "You have for a long time. You're seeing that sex doctor next week just so I won't leave."

I remind him of what Joan said about that. But he's on a roll.

"You never buy me nice birthday gifts. It's like an afterthought to you. I tell you things, ask you to do things, and you never listen to me."

"That's bullshit! You're just making up stuff! *You* never listen to *me!*"

We're like a broken record stuck in the same dysfunctional groove. We're two five-year-old's, fighting over the same ratty toy. We're a dog licking a hot spot. We're a really bad metaphor. When our spat subsides, Mark sends an email to the workshop coordinator asking if addiction will be addressed. An automatic email response says we should expect a screening call. The next morning, he hugs me in the kitchen.

"I'm going through some internal struggles right now." *No shit.*

Mark wonders aloud if some of the problem might be related to his going off his antidepressant. I want to say that maybe he should get back on it. But I don't.

"Love you," he says, kissing me goodbye.

The next day, he criticizes me for several minor issues. I write them down and read them back to him. In the next breath, he tells me he loves me and wants to work things out. I have become a human pin cushion. It has to stop. That night, I keep my voice even in the kitchen.

"I know you're going through some stuff, but this back and forth isn't fair to me."

Mark listens. Then he says, "They say to give your marriage one full year when your spouse gets sober. You're only six months in." Right.

"I want to know how you're feeling, but this back and forth has to stop." I repeat. "It's getting hard on me."

Okay, he says. We sign up for the marriage workshop the following weekend in Dallas. A day or so passes. Suddenly, Mark's anger vanishes. "What's going on?" I ask.

"I have been praying about it, and I think it's helped me gain some clarity."

Until the next wave comes, I think.

Chapter Twenty-Six

The marriage workshop is held in a large room with several rows of chairs inside an office building off the main freeway. The teachers are a dark-haired, zaftig woman and a slouchy, pasty guy—a married couple who are trained Gottman disciples. There are more than a dozen other couples, each toting their Gottman workbooks. Danish trays rest on a table, and coffee percolates. We all take our seats.

The couple talks about good and bad marriages, stuff we've already read in the book. Really, we could have saved ourselves the $500. We go through written and oral exercises. Then we're instructed to scatter about in a leafy courtyard to work together on a series of questions. Some of them are downright goofy. Mark and I collapse in laughter, turning the exercise into a joke, which is what we do when we're at our healthiest. At one point, we glance around the courtyard. Most of the other couples are serious and somber, with their heads bowed over the worksheets. A wife or two is crying. *Maybe we aren't so bad off after all.*

During an afternoon break, we retreat to our car to escape the earnestness. I put my bare feet up on the dashboard. We're both full and drowsy from the turkey-sub lunch and from sitting all day in the classroom. We slide our seats into recline. A soft breeze blows through the open windows.

"When I was little, my mother would go into rages," Mark says, his voice sounding far away. "All the stress of five kids, I guess. She couldn't handle it. She'd take her pack of cigarettes and leave, saying she was never coming back. She did it more than once. I'd start cleaning the house, looking out the window every few minutes to see if she'd come back. I think the cleaning was my way of trying to get a sense of order in what felt like total chaos."

I picture Mark as a little boy, staring out that window. It breaks my heart.

"No wonder my messiness freaks you out. I'm sorry. I'm going to try and do better."

We're quiet for a minute or so. The vague drone of the nearby freeway sounds like waves on the beach. "I'm sorry for all those times I got mad at you for your drinking," Mark says.

"What about the enabling?"

"I'm sorry for that, too."

The breeze curls around our conversation, gently pushing our words to a protected space. A place free of animosity or blame.

"I'm sorry it took me so long to get sober. I took advantage of the situation. I hurt you and Sam. I'm going to spend the rest of my life making it up to you both."

Mark reaches out his hand to me. I slide my own into it. His palm feels warm and strong.

"All I know is that I love you, and I'm committed to staying with you, no matter what," he says.

"I feel the same way."

It's almost time to go back into the classroom.

"We're going to have to find a new way to be together," I say. "Drinking was such a big part of our relationship. Now there's this big hole that we used to fill with drinking together. We don't have that anymore."

Mark yawns, stretches out his long frame, the one I fell in love with the moment I first spied him stretched out on his friend's couch, wearing the orange sweater he bought for our first date.

"I know. It's scary. But it's also kind of exciting," he says.

I lean over, brush back the scrim of dark hair that falls over his forehead.

"I feel like we're having to get to know each other for the first time. Maybe that's what all this static has been about. We're starting to actually have a real relationship."

"I'm game to keep going if you are," Mark says.

"I'm totally game."

We roll up the windows. Lean into each other, kiss.

A few weeks later, we go to a game night at the home of some new sober friends we've met. Somebody makes the comment "Everybody wins!" after a certain move is made on the board game we're playing. Soon, we're all exclaiming, "Everybody wins!" after each move, throwing our arms up in the air as if we're doing the wave at a baseball game. We're all cutting up, cracking jokes, practically falling out of our chairs laughing.

"Man, I didn't know you could have so much fun without drinking," Mark says, snaking his arm around my waist as we walk to the car.

We start having regular "date nights," going out to eat each Friday night, then catching a film at an art-house theater near our neighborhood.

"You're so much better to talk to now," Mark says, loading up a chip with guacamole at one of our date dinners. "You're funnier and smarter than you were back then."

"And you're slowly becoming less of an asshole," I say, winking and giving him a broad, sugary smile.

On our thirtieth anniversary, when I am five years sober, we take a three-week trip to Italy and London that proves to be the experience of a lifetime. We traipse through piazzas, museums, and churches, holding hands, marveling at centuries-old landmarks and art. The trip is forever burned in my memory and my heart, crisp and sharp, because that's how my brain works now.

My sobriety had marked the beginning of a new phase in our marriage. One that would bring us together as the two people we really were, instead of the two stand-ins created by the mediating filter of alcohol. After more than three decades together, we began a slow climb out of old patterns to stand on a stronger platform, one that enabled us to love one another at a depth we never dreamed possible.

Our old pattern of fighting and then not talking to each other for hours—days, even—happened a handful of times and then sputtered to a stop.

For a while, we had Joan on speed dial. I imagined her sighing whenever she saw our number in her incoming call box. Tune-ups, we called them. Those finally stopped, too. We didn't need them anymore.

Not that we never bickered again. Humans are humans. Real intimacy sometimes has rough edges. But that day in the car at the Gottman retreat marked the start of our true marriage, a journey that would be graced with more laughter, love, and just plain fun than all that had come before.

Oh, and the sex. Doing it sober was weird at first, which wasn't surprising. Across the totality of my sexual life, from my teens up to and including my marriage, I rarely had intercourse without first ingesting at least some alcohol to loosen me up, to create a buffer zone. In sobriety, that was out the window. Having sex with Mark at first felt awkward, almost robotic. The smells and sensations were a little too real. But then I got used to it, and then it got better. *A lot better.* Which made it happen more often. Who said post-menopausal women can't rock a randy sex life?

Sex wasn't the only surprise. My concern all along had been that no alcohol would translate into no pleasure at all. A boring, dry existence. But in fact, I've found more pleasure in sobriety. No, it's not the outsized, not-found-in-nature, fake dopamine-dump euphoria of alcohol. I'm talking more about the earth-bound, garden-variety, sensual pleasure that comes from simply being alive. The humid smell right before a rainstorm. The first sip of hot morning coffee. The endorphin updraft after a brisk walk. The thrill of coming home to find a copy of the New Yorker in my mailbox. The therapeutic delight of burying my fingers in the dirt. Released from my disease, I discovered I have an affinity for growing things; my front porch and back deck soon bloomed with a profusion of flowers and greenery. My writing at work became reinvigorated.

I decided to set down my alcoholism experiences in a memoir, hoping someone out there might relate. Might be helped.

Mark, too, discovered a rich vein of creativity once his untreated Al-Anon-ism went into remission. (If our story demonstrates anything, it's that untreated loved ones of alcoholics can be just as sick as the drinker. Perhaps sicker.) In my third year of sobriety, Mark picked up his stained-glass tools again. Soon, almost every window of our home shone with color and geometric designs. He took up mosaic; just about every tabletop and mirror in our house over time was encrusted with vibrant tile. (The running joke is that if I'm stationary too long, Mark might mosaic me!)

It's perhaps one of the biggest gifts of sobriety. Most of the time, I go through life feeling happy. Stupidly happy. Happy for no reason. A vegetable happiness.

And all I wanted was to stop drinking.

Chapter Twenty-Seven

Meanwhile, Sam had been living in Austin for about a year, waiting tables at an Italian restaurant, deciding what he was going to do with his life. The week I left rehab, Mark and I drove to his house in Austin to take him and his roommates to lunch. Before we left their house, I pulled Sam into a bedroom and made my formal amends to him. It was a stilted, two-minute conversation: my son had heard my apologies before. "Okay, Mom," he said. "Thanks for the amends." Then we went to lunch. A year or so later, I would learn from Katie, one of his high school friends, that Sam didn't trust my recovery until I reached one year of sobriety. Then he began to let out the breath he'd been holding since high school.

Before I hit one year of sobriety, Sam moved back home so he could save up money for graduate school. He'd been accepted into the master's degree program in English at New York University. Having him live with us for a handful of months felt like a minor miracle, a gift from the Universe: *I get to show him I'm sober, not just say I am.* One day, he stands in the doorway of the den.

"Mom, will you shave my head?" He's holding a special set of electric clippers he borrowed from a friend.

"You bet." I put down my book and we go into his bathroom. Sam sits on the closed toilet.

"Just run it evenly over my head," he instructs.

I run the razor back and forth over my son's head, his lustrous light brown curls dropping to the floor, the razor making a comforting hum. This is the most I've been able to touch him in years, apart from our seconds-long hugs upon greeting or goodbye-ing. I revel in this small act of caring and wonder—*would Sam have trusted me with the razor if I was still drinking?*

Slowly, our relationship thaws, then warms up. But whenever Sam is surly or short with me, I think: *Is it because I drank?*

In the not-too-distant future, Sam will tell me that, yes, some of his anger had been a holdover from my drinking. He didn't drink his first year of college because of what he'd been through with me and he experienced some depression. I will apologize again and tell him it's normal for children of alcoholics to carry around that turmoil. He will apologize too, for his anger, which will cleave my heart in two. At first, his words will hurt, but then I'll realize: we're talking openly about my drinking and the damage it caused, and that can't be anything but healing.

In the years to come, when Sam lives in Houston while he works on a PhD in English at Rice University, he'll make regular visits home. He and I will sit in the kitchen and drink glass bottles of Topo Chico while he cooks a vegetarian feast. We'll have long, discursive conversations about politics and religion, art and writing, and I will wonder anew: *Would these dialogues be happening if I was still drinking? Almost certainly not.*

What a gift —what a priceless gift.

If I could wave a magic wand and remove all the pain that I caused my son, I would. But I can't. So my hope—my prayer—is that one day he'll be able to take the pain I inflicted and somehow transform it into something good. Because that's the only point of all that pain that I can see.

Back in the bathroom, I finish shaving Sam's head. We admire his newly shorn scalp in the mirror.

"Good job, Mom."

"You're lucky you have a nicely shaped head."

"I do?" He turns side to side, checking out his new look. Then he kisses me on the cheek. I stow away this tiny jewel in what is becoming a growing cache of precious stones: *I am a good mother.*

Something else amazing happens.

One day, I'm just sitting there, maybe in my recliner at home, at my desk at work, or in my car at a red light, and yet another realization hits: just like my craving to drink, my obsession with what others think of me has somehow... stopped. The space between bouts of ruminating about *not being good enough* and spaces of peace has gradually stretched longer and longer until not worrying has become more prevalent than worrying. The rule instead of the exception. It feels like when a neighbor's loud music suddenly stops, and the ensuing silence is stark, noticeable.

Every now and then, I slip back into obsessing. But I don't stew in it anymore. I don't bubble and ooze like an overripe tomato.

There's a saying in recovery: We often don't see the changes in ourselves as readily as others do because we're too close to the transformation. I knew I'd made significant strides when Rich, one nosy co-worker of mine who'd always loved teasing me (a favorite was telling me he'd heard a rumor I was about to be fired) made a casual observation on the way back from lunch one day. "I can't gig you anymore," he said. "You don't react like you used to."

I grinned back at him.

Margaret taught me a cool trick by way of Eckhart Tolle: distance yourself from the voices in your head. Watch them.

Observe them. Just the watching seems to turn down the heat.

The $1 million question:

Did God really bring all this about? My ability to stop drinking? My release from constant worrying? My greatly expanded life? A rejuvenated creativity? More authentic relationships? Or was it all the work of a great sponsor, a great therapist, and the amazing fellowship I found?

Hell if I know. I've decided it doesn't matter. Fifteen years in, it's hard to argue with success.

"It's through our common pain that we heal together," Margaret told me in the first year of my sobriety. "You're going to sponsor a woman one day who worries all the time about what others think, and you'll be able to say, 'I know exactly what you mean.'"

*   *   *

The opportunity comes sooner than I expected.

It's a blustery Sunday. I decide to attend a newcomers' meeting at Club 12. I'm about to hit one year of sobriety. Margaret and Joan have been encouraging —pestering—me to raise my hand in meetings when the chair asks if anyone is willing to be a sponsor. It's time, they say. You're ready. *You only get to keep what you give away.* The idea of sponsoring someone sets my nerves jangling. *Who am I to help another person become sober?* It's only recently that I've begun to get my own ridiculous road show together.

As I sit in Club 12, the rumble of approaching thunder can be heard. It's a big group, about fifty people. The rule in newcomers' meetings is that you can only share if you have six months of sobriety or less. One by one, folks slumped in chairs share stories about the perils of early sobriety, how hard it is not to pick up a drink in those first shaky months. At one point, a pretty Latina woman raises her hand. She wears a bandana on her head, tamping down her dark black curls.

It's been a struggle, she says, her arm curled around the back of her chair. She knows she has to stop drinking or she might lose her husband and son. (A shiver of recognition makes me listen hard.) She needs to find a sponsor and start working the steps. Working up my courage, I approach her after the meeting as people mill about, shake hands, and chat.

"I only have about a year, but I'm willing to take you on if you're interested," I say. I feel like a boy in junior high asking her to the dance.

"You'll be my guinea pig. I've never sponsored anyone before." The woman smiles. Her lips twitch a teeny bit.

"Do you smoke?" she says. "Want to go outside and have a cigarette and discuss it?"

"You bet."

We stand outside the entrance, under a narrow alcove. As we light our cigarettes, flashes of lightning streak across the darkened afternoon sky followed by rolling booms of thunder. Gusts of wind throw dirt and trash around the parking lot. Big, fat raindrops start to fall. The woman tells me her name is Marina. She's in her thirties, a social worker, and a nightly wine drinker. She's never tried to get sober before. There was a recent ugly incident where she passed out on her front lawn during a blackout, frightening her pre-teen son. It's made her determined to give the program a try. She's desperate, actually. I give her the broad outlines of my story. Now the rain is coming down hard, sheets of water blowing sideways, the only thing keeping us from getting drenched is the shelter of the alcove. We're both nervous, laughing and talking fast—the words tumbling out, scared and excited to have found each other. Marina tells me she's a people-pleaser who worries obsessively about what others think of her. She fears her drinking has hurt her son, and she's resentful that her husband continues to drink as she tries to get sober.

I shit you not. *Here it is*, I thought, *the pain that unites.*

"I can relate to a lot of what you're saying," I yell over the downpour.

"OK," she yells back. "OK. I want you to be my sponsor."

Marina becomes the first woman I shepherd through the 12 Steps. In the years that follow, she'll be joined by other women—a schoolteacher, a Presbyterian minister, a hard-charging attorney. Each had arrived at the same conclusion, that great gift: to drink is to die.

Not long after I meet Marina, I'm driving to one of my last aftercare sessions with Dr. B. I have a strong urge to call my new sponsee on my cell to share some little piece of wisdom I've just learned from Margaret that I think will help her. I look at my car's digital clock as I speed up the hill to Dr. B's office. I don't know if I have enough time. She might want to talk, and group starts in five minutes. What should I do? I feel an urgency but decide to wait. I'll call her later.

As I climb out of my car, one of those little epiphanies—in a year full of epiphanies—strikes me. A year ago around this time of day, with the sun sinking low on the horizon and my craving for wine kicking into high gear, I would have been debating a far different dilemma: How much wine can I sneak tonight? How drunk can I get without getting into trouble? Not, how can I help a recovering alcoholic live a better life? I smile and click the auto-lock on my car key.

This is better.

Far, far better.

Epilogue

Mark and I sit in the car outside a clapboard building on the outskirts of Seguin, a rural south Texas town forty-five minutes east of San Antonio. It's nighttime. The lights of the interstate twinkle off in the distance. An irregular line of blackbirds rests suspended on telephone wires above our heads.

We're here to tell our story about how drinking brought us together, and how my sobriety almost tore us apart. This isn't the first time we've done a tandem presentation at a 12-Step meeting, with Mark sharing his perspective and me sharing mine. In my second year of sobriety, we did our little dog-and-pony show at Club 12. I've had to overcome a strong fear of public speaking to do this work. According to unofficial recovery dogma, when someone asks you to do service work—to speak, to act as someone's sponsor, whatever—the best answer is always "yes."

So here we are.

We're feeling a bit like fish out of water. We've never been to this meeting before. A row of Harleys is lined up outside this Seguin 12-Step club, along with a smattering of run-down vehicles. A bunch of rough-looking dudes smoke under the yellow porch light. There's nothing else around but rows of darkened farm fields.

But, really, there's no cause to be afraid. Because it doesn't matter where a meeting happens. Be it an upscale suburban church, downtown office building, or remote rural outpost, the texture and tone are always the same. It doesn't matter if those gathered are poor, rich, Black, White, brown, gay, straight, Republican, Democrat (and in the fellowship, it's often a mixture of all the above, *how cool is that?*). You pretty much know going in what you're going to get: understanding, acceptance, and an abiding sense of not being alone.

And it's all free, except for the dollar you throw in the basket, or don't throw, no one's going to judge you.

People who don't have a drinking problem ("normies," as we call them in the program) would be shocked to discover how much laughter goes on at 12-Step meetings. Real, authentic, balls-out laughter. And how little time is spent talking about drinking, although of course, there's some of that. The focus tends to be on living in the moment. On how to move through the world practicing the principles of the program: Patience. Tolerance. Compassion. Gratitude. Honesty.

On how to keep living your life doing *the next right thing.*

There's a lot of laughter in meetings because we're all alcoholics, and we like to feel good, and because we know that, as a group, we've slipped the noose of death and degradation, as long as we keep doing a few simple things. The Big Book calls it the laughter of people who've grabbed onto the lifebuoy, who've made it onto the lifeboat.

Part of how we do that is by telling each other our stories.

God with skin on, as the saying goes.

"Well, this looks promising," Mark says, watching as a heavily tattooed man flicks away his cigarette and enters the building.

"Yep, should be an interesting crowd." Mark turns off the car and looks at me.

"You ready?"

"As I'll ever be."

We get out of the car, clasp hands, and go inside.

Acknowledgements

Like sobriety, writing a book takes a community. For two years, I journeyed to Austin once a month to take part in Ron Seybold's Writer's Workshop, where I sat around a table with our merry band of fellow memoirists to nail down the contours of my story. Ron, Leesa Ross, Anne Bayerkohler, and Dave Barstow – your fingerprints are all over this book. Without your encouragement, support, and writerly wisdom – and all the laughing, we can't forget the laughing – my recovery story would have remained a museum piece in my head.

Thank you to Julene Franki, another memoirist and fabulous painter, for blowing a fresh gust of wind into my sails when I was about to abandon ship. Without seeing you at that party, where you kicked my ass back into gear, I would have given up.

Mil gracias to my professor friend and poet extraordinaire Catherine Bowman, for the unceasing propping-up you gave me through the years as I struggled to write this book and find a publisher. Cathy, your thoughts on writing and storytelling are like precious gems to me, as is our long friendship. I will love you until the end of time.

I don't know if I have enough words to thank Usher Morgan, CEO of Library Tales Publishing, who pulled my manuscript from the slush pile and immediately "got" why, yes, the world might indeed need another recovery memoir. Thanks also to LTP's crackerjack copy editor Sydney DellaRatta, for tightening the ship and making it more seaworthy.

Thanks to Joan Ellis, the best therapist around—and I've seen lots of therapists; you stuck with us during that tempestuous first year of my sobriety, when my husband and I had your number on speed dial.

Unending gratitude and endless hosannas to "Margaret," also known as Cathy Daily (who gave me permission to break her anonymity), my "sponsor from heaven," who threw me a life buoy right as I was drowning. Cathy, you helped save my marriage and quite possibly my life, and I will forever cherish the fact we've become dear friends as well as sober sisters.

To my steadfast spouse Mark – thank you for reading multiple versions of the Drunk Love manuscript as it morphed over the years, and for never once asking me to pretty things up or make you look better. You're the best Al-Anon a recovered drunk could ever hope for, and I love you in this life and the next. (Also, thanks for not divorcing me.)

Thank you to my brave grown offspring Sam, for also reading this book pre-publication and for not flinching at the hard parts, and for loving your mother through both her illness and her health. I'm enormously proud of you. The fact that we've healed past my disease is perhaps the greatest part of my sobriety journey and attests to the hope and restoration to be found in recovery.

Finally, and perhaps most importantly, I wish to thank the men and women of the 12-Step fellowship to which I belong, for your experience, strength, and hope, but mostly for your stories.